Praise for
I Like Giving

"Important and exciting! *I Like Giving* could be the beginning of a movement of generosity."
> —MARK BATTERSON, author of *The Circle Maker*

"*I Like Giving* will light you up on the generosity dial."
> —DAVE RAMSEY, host of *The Dave Ramsey Show* and
> *New York Times* best-selling author

"*I Like Giving* inspires us to explore giving that is full of cheer and joy. These stories have opened up our eyes to see our daily interactions with people in a whole new way."
> —DAVID and BARBARA GREEN, cofounders of
> Hobby Lobby

"*I Like Giving* is a beautifully written book with the right title, because people really do like giving. Brad Formsma has an inspiring message, and his book should be on every kitchen table, like a daily vitamin for the soul."
> —STEPHEN POST, best-selling author of *Why*
> *Good Things Happen to Good People*

"Brad's understanding of generosity is a wake-up call for the giver inside us all."
> —MICHAEL JR., award-winning comedian

THE TRANSFORMING POWER OF A GENEROUS LIFE

I LIKE GIVING

PRACTICAL IDEAS, INSPIRING STORIES

BRAD FORMSMA

WATERBROOK

I LIKE GIVING

The Scripture quotation is taken from the Holy Bible, New Living Translation, copyright © 1996, 2004, 2007. Used by permission of Tyndale House Publishers Inc., Carol Stream, Illinois 60188. All rights reserved.

Details and names in some anecdotes and stories have been changed to protect the identities of the persons involved.

"The Paradoxical Commandments" are reprinted with the permission of the author. © Copyright Kent M. Keith 1968, renewed 2001.

Trade Paperback ISBN 978-1-60142-575-1
eBook ISBN 978-1-60142-576-8

Copyright © 2014 by Brad Formsma
Photos © by I Like Giving; photography by Carson David Brown

Cover design: Baas Creative

Published in association with the literary agency of The Fedd Agency Inc., P.O. Box 341973, Austin, TX 78734.

Published in the United States by WaterBrook, an imprint of the Crown Publishing Group, a division of Penguin Random House LLC, New York.

WATERBROOK and its deer colophon are registered trademarks of Penguin Random House LLC.

Library of Congress Cataloging-in-Publication Data
Formsma, Brad.
    I like giving : the transforming power of a generous life : practical ideas, inspiring stories / Brad Formsma. — First Edition.
        pages cm
    ISBN 978-1-60142-575-1 — ISBN 978-1-60142-576-8 1. Generosity—Religious aspects—Christianity. I. Title.
    BV4647.G45F67 2014
    241'.4—dc23

                                                    2013038961

Printed in the United States of America
2019

20 19 18 17 16 15 14

SPECIAL SALES
Most WaterBrook books are available at special quantity discounts when purchased in bulk by corporations, organizations, and special-interest groups. Custom imprinting or excerpting can also be done to fit special needs. For information, please e-mail specialmarketscms@penguinrandomhouse.com or call 1-800-603-7051.

To my wife, Laura,
who knew this book would happen
years before it did.
Without you and your encouragement,
this book would never have come to pass.

I love you.

● ● ●

CONTENTS

WHAT'S YOUR STORY?

Stories hold the power to transform our view of ourselves and our place in the world. They can propel us to action, inspiring us to plow through the roadblocks we set and the excuses we tell. The right story can change your life. More than that, it can help you change the lives of others.

In this book you hold a collection of incredible, real-life stories about normal people choosing to be generous with their words, attention, money, influence, possessions, and time. These are stories of everyday people who overcame all the usual excuses: *I can start to be generous when I'm more established. I'm too poor to give. Right now I need to focus on myself and my family. Generous acts don't matter unless they are grand.*

In each story you'll discover that living generously is easy. Really! Humans are hardwired for it. When we give, our brains release beneficial hormones and lift our moods. We feel more open, more alive, and more grateful. Moreover, our generosity ripples outward, improving the lives of others—sometimes in ways we would never dare imagine.

The stories within these pages will challenge you to think differently about giving. They will inspire you to live generously today, right where you are. You'll find yourself looking for opportunities while you wait in line at Starbucks or while stuck in a traffic jam. You'll be encouraged to give in the lunchroom at work or in the kitchen at home. Follow the lead in these stories and start making simple, everyday choices that provide joy, purpose, and excitement—for yourself *and* for others.

A life of giving isn't focused on what we have to do or should do; it's an adventure we get to join! It's a story we get to write—and if your life tells the right story, how many other lives will it change?

1

THE POWER OF
ONE GIFT

The giving journey for Tracy Autler started on Thanksgiving Day 1993. Away from her family, living in an apartment on the lower end of town, a single mom to a three-year-old and eight months pregnant, she was relying on welfare and food stamps to get by. While other families were preparing for their Thanksgiving feasts, Tracy would do the best she could with canned food.

Standing in her apartment and looking at the sparse collection of cans on her shelf, Tracy heard a knock at the door. *What in the world?* she thought. Who would be coming to her door on Thanksgiving Day? Weren't people at home with their families, eating turkey and watching football? She opened her door and simply couldn't believe her eyes.

Standing there was a man from a local restaurant with a delivery for Tracy: a full Thanksgiving dinner, complete with all the trimmings. He said it was from an anonymous donor, and before Tracy could ask any questions, he handed it over and left. Tracy was so overwhelmed that she spent the rest of the day crying.

Surprised and amazed, Tracy decided she needed to know whom to thank for this extravagant and timely gift. However, she couldn't figure it out. She called her parents, but it wasn't them. She asked her friends, but no one knew. Tracy couldn't believe that someone outside her circle of friends and family had noticed her situation and done something about it without drawing any attention to himself.

Years went by, and Tracy still had no idea whom the mysterious Thanksgiving dinner had come from. In time she moved out of that apartment and began working as a nurse at a local hospital.

And then it happened. Seven years after that special Thanksgiving meal, a woman named Margot was admitted into Tracy's care. Margot had multiple sclerosis, and her condition was becoming critical. Tracy remembered Margot from her time on welfare. She had lived in the same apartment building as Tracy. It was clear that Margot didn't have much longer to live.

Three days before her death, Margot took Tracy's hand in hers and, in a frail voice, whispered two words: "Happy Thanksgiving."

In that moment Tracy knew who had given her that Thanksgiving dinner. She would never have guessed that

Margot—the unassuming neighbor with multiple sclerosis—was behind that generous gift. Tracy still gets tears in her eyes when she tells the story today.

I'd call that story "I Like My Neighbor." Margot saw Tracy's situation that Thanksgiving Day and did something extraordinary—she gave her the perfect gift without anyone asking her to and without asking for anything in return.

That one gift had a massive impact on Tracy's life.

Moved by the anonymous donor's generosity, Tracy purposed in her heart to do generous things for other people too. The very day she got off assistance, she took a basket of gifts down to the welfare office for anyone to take. The welfare officer was stunned. Can you imagine the look on his face? Who does something like that?

And that was just the beginning. Since then, Tracy and her husband have become foster parents and adopted a son. She regularly looks for opportunities to give. The last time I heard from her, she was getting ready to volunteer her Saturday afternoon at the local Humane Society. One of her latest ideas is to leave five-dollar Starbucks gift cards with little notes for her coworkers to find, just to make their day better. This year Tracy and her family made a New Year's resolution to find one hundred opportunities to give to other people. How inspiring is that?

What I appreciate most about Tracy is that she doesn't do her giving to be noticed by others. Since that Thanksgiving Day in 1993, she has discovered the joy that comes from giving. Now she's hooked. She doesn't give to make herself look good—she gives because she *likes* giving. It makes her feel more alive. "It's how life should be," she says.

● ● ●

There is something incredible about giving when it's our idea. Opening our eyes and ears to the people around us and asking "How can we give?" is a profoundly life-giving and satisfying way to live. One of Jesus's ideas was that it is more blessed to give than to receive. I have found that to be true. The generous life is the only life worth living.

Just imagine—what if every single person on the planet woke up and, like Tracy, looked for ways to give? What sort of world could we create through the simple, powerful decision to live generously? Whoever you are, no matter how much or how little you have to share, making the decision to give regularly to others—daily, weekly, or monthly—will enrich your life and change the lives of the people around you.

When we choose to give, we change, and the people around us change. When we move from awareness to action, miracles happen. When we allow giving to be our idea, a world of possibilities opens up before us, and we discover new levels of joy. If you, like Tracy, get hooked on giving, you'll find yourself asking, "How generous can I be?" When that happens, you'll realize that, not only are you loving life more than ever, but you're also a part of creating a more generous world—a world that is better for all of us.

If you haven't ever experienced the joy of giving, or it's been a long time, this book will show you where to start. We will walk with you as you take your first steps, and we'll stick with you as you grow in the art of generosity.

Or if you're nodding your head right now, saying, "I've known this for years," then we're here to encourage you to keep growing and to empower you to spread the joy. We never arrive. I've been discovering the joy of generous living for many years, and I still feel as if I'm just getting started!

The best things in life are like that—they grow and never end.

I LIKE WILLIAM.

Submitted by: Elizabeth

In the affluent Ivy League town of Princeton, New Jersey, someone like William tends to stick out from the crowd. William is sixty-seven years old, and, as is evident from his personal appearance, he has a disability. William has cerebral palsy. Our family had become aware of William because we'd seen him riding around town on his scooter, but mostly we knew William because he swept the sidewalk and opened the door for customers at Starbucks, my local coffee oasis.

Being a bit of a coffee addict, I tend to frequent the Starbucks in downtown Princeton, often going there with my family. From the beginning, we noticed William and took time to get to know him. My three-year-old, Chase, gets especially excited whenever we see William's scooter outside. Over the past year or so, William has become our friend.

Recently, however, I realized William had a need we could not see. His eyes were bad. I discovered this one Saturday as I sat working on my laptop. My boys weren't with me this time, so when William came by, I took more time than usual to talk with him and get to know him better.

After we'd been talking awhile, I began to show him some family pictures on our laptop. To my amazement William couldn't see them even though they were right in front of his face!

I asked William if he had glasses. As it turned out, he had a pair, but he had accidentally sat on them, and they were ruined. I had work to do, and putting off William's situation would have been the easy choice, but I felt compelled to act. I called LensCrafters and made an appointment for three o'clock that same day.

When I got home and announced my plan to the family, my husband laughed kindly at me—he's not too surprised when I do things like this—and rearranged his schedule so we could take William to the eye doctor as a family. When three o'clock rolled around, we picked up William from Starbucks and, with the kids in tow, headed over to get his eyes checked.

The optometrist at LensCrafters picked up on what we were doing and showed special kindness to William. He confirmed that William's eyes were, in fact, very bad and made a new pair of glasses for him.

We're very happy to know that William will be able to see well again, especially as he rides his scooter around town!

Every year I choose one word to focus on for the upcoming year. This year my word was *give*. While I feel I give my life away every day in caring for two young boys, I have felt less able to give to my community since becoming a mom. Having the opportunity to help William get glasses not only gave me a way to practice giving, but because we knew him, it also fostered our relationship with him and our connection to our community.

My faith moved me to help William promptly. I believe that we are called to love everyone, even "the least of these." In many ways William, a poor disabled man, is disadvantaged in Princeton. It filled me with so much joy that I was able to be a blessing to him in a time of need and model giving to my kids in a fresh way. I am grateful to have a part in improving William's life.

2
BEGINNINGS

My first encounter with generosity came early in life when I was a kid tagging along behind my grandfather. He owned a large commercial bakery. On Saturdays I would often accompany him to his work. It made me feel important to help him out.

Together we would bake a dozen loaves of bread. He knew the recipe by heart. Once the loaves were in the oven, it was my job to keep an eye on them while he took care of business matters. By midafternoon we would take a drive and give the bread we had baked together to people and families around town.

Grandpa had his tough side too, but when it came to giving, his generosity extended way beyond bread. I remember being in his office one Saturday when he took out a list and showed it to me with a gleam in his eye. It was a list of people and organizations that he gave money to over the course of the year. To me, an eleven-year-old kid, the total at the bottom of the list seemed like a lot! Looking me in the eye, he said, "Giving is good, and God often brings it back so you can do it again." Years later when my grandpa passed away, I found a note he had written to me when I was fourteen. It said, "Brad, Winston Churchill said you make a living by what you earn and a life by what you give. I thought this would be well worth remembering. Love, Gramps."

He had no idea how prophetic that note would turn out to be.

You see, I wasn't always as excited about giving as I am today. Sure, I gave a little here and there, but for the most part, my life had always been about me. I figured out at a young age that things weren't going to be handed to me, so as a teenager I started my own business, mowing lawns. The business grew as I entered college, and soon I found myself splitting my days between it, school, and a job at the local Olive Garden restaurant. Waiting tables gave me fast cash to put toward equipment payments for my business. I was enjoying the early rewards of hard work.

While I was serving tables at the Olive Garden, one of my regular diners introduced me to her daughter, Laura. We soon started dating, and now, after twenty years of marriage, we're thankful Laura's mom knew a good match when she saw one!

We both graduated from college and quickly settled

into living the American Dream. Laura loved teaching first grade, and I had a now-blossoming landscape business to run. My business had expanded to include construction and heavy equipment, and it was doing exceptionally well. With all the money that was coming in, we became really good at giving to ourselves while giving just a little to others.

We both had grown up going to church, but our faith had never really been a big part of our lives. If you had asked me back then, I would have said I believed in God and in doing things to help others, but the reality was that I was often motivated by selfish ambition. I enjoyed being successful in business and was hungry for more money, position, and prestige.

Then our first son, Danny, came into the world, and everything changed.

We met others through church who had just had children and found a peace in their lives that appealed to us. We found ourselves wanting to be part of something bigger than creating our own perfect lifestyle.

To this day I vividly remember the moment during that time when I realized I wanted to take my faith more seriously. I was driving home from work one day and said, "Wherever you are, take over my life, and I'll do what you want me to do." I wasn't sure if I was talking to myself or if someone really heard what I said.

Something happened that day, to be honest, because things have never been the same.

Laura and I began to invest more in our faith. When it came to business, however, I was still very driven by money. My heart motivation was in a bad place. I often put myself in situations where I could become a partner or investor in projects, thinking that leveraging what I had would get me ahead. The landscape business was booming, but I was still hungry for more. Frankly, greed led me to make business decisions I would later regret.

A client approached me with financial projections for a business deal that seemed like a cash cow—we'd be able to pay off our house, send our kids to college, and drive the perfect car from the profit we'd turn. I jumped right in.

Bad call. The opportunity I had hoped would be a massive moneymaker instead became one of the worst business decisions of my life. A significant amount of money was lost, and I was charged with liquidating the assets.

That wasn't the only deal that went south. I was on a hot streak. Another investment that seemed like a sure thing ended in disappointment, and other moneymaking opportunities and so-called investments became nothing more than weights around my neck. I finally realized that, even though I had decided to live a life of faith, it was greed that was motivating these decisions and controlling my life. Of course, I never would have said that at the time. Greed took on the guise of wanting to grow a business, of seeking success. Ultimately, it was a lack of contentment.

It was a humbling thing to admit my true motives, but once I did, the new awareness not only felt good, but it also helped me avoid making similar mistakes in the future. What I eventually realized was that through these spoiled business ventures, God was working on my heart.

A few years went by, and Drew was born. Then we had our third child, a daughter—Grace. We were again thankful for God's generous gift of life.

We were also starting to give in a totally new way. Burned out by a sense of duty that I felt whenever I was asked to give, I started looking for ways to give that were in line with my heart. For some reason an organization doing relief work in India caught my attention. One day I sat down, wrote them a generous check, and sent it to them. It felt great! No one had told me to give to that organization—it was my idea—and because my heart was in it, I felt joy in being able to help.

Laura also found ways to give that were in line with her heart, and as she did, our joy increased. Our kids even got in on the action and started surprising us with their generosity. Embracing generosity as a lifestyle started to give us joy and satisfaction and brought a whole new dimension to our family.

What was happening to us?

We were discovering the excitement of giving because it was our idea.

This way of giving brought with it such a good feeling that I started to look for other opportunities to give in everyday life. Sometimes I'd go to the store and look for an elderly person counting her coupons; I'd be sure to give her a handshake, and as she took my hand, she'd find some money in it. Other times I would sneak up behind someone and give the cashier money toward the person's groceries before making a hasty escape.

It was contagious. We fell in love with giving, whether it was at the store, in a restaurant, or through our daily lives.

Before we became givers, our lives were pretty empty. We were living the American Dream and were good at it, but it turned out to be more of a nightmare than a dream. Ultimately, it was superficial. When your life is just about your next restaurant dinner, the next remodeling project, or the next lifestyle upgrade, it's not that rich. Sure, money can buy things, but money can't buy joy.

Joy doesn't come from filling your life with stuff.

Joy comes from giving your life away.

In 2005 I was reading a book that explained how God speaks to us today. This was news to me, but I thought I'd give it a try. With some trepidation I went out on a run and found myself asking, *Well, if it's true that you speak to people, what would you like to say to me?* There on that dirt road, I had a strong impression that God replied. In a mysterious way I had the sense that I was being moved to encourage people in their giving and that I would have the opportunity to influence many people toward greater life and joy.

Later that year I received a business achievement award. When a person from the publication that gave the award came to interview me, she asked me a simple question: If I could have my dream job, what would it be? I almost surprised myself with my response: "I would love to encourage people in their giving because I believe we live in a self-focused world, and that conflicts with my belief that it is more blessed to give than to receive."

I didn't know it at the time, but my life was about to change.

Within a year of that article, a friend introduced me to an organization that is privately funded. I soon attended a gathering the organization held in the Detroit area. The event simply brought people together to challenge them to consider what it means to be generous.

I was so energized by the organization and its purpose that I began to volunteer some of my time to it. Before long, they asked if I might be interested in serving with them in an official capacity. I was in.

It was an emotional moment for me as I could sense the hand of God in the events of my life. My interest in the business I had created from scratch now paled in comparison with my enthusiasm for this new work of encouraging people to give. I felt like I had a new lease on life.

For a while I ran my business part-time and served in the nonprofit world part-time. It soon became clear, however, that I was spread too thin. Laura and I took some time to think and pray, and we concluded that we should sell the business. I still remember sitting across the dinner table from Laura's dad and feeling very uncomfortable as he said, "Let me get this right. You're selling your business so you can go work for a nonprofit?" The response from our friends was similar, and we honestly didn't know if we would have to sell our home or move our kids to a different school as a result of this career change. It was a scary decision, but we knew that our hearts were no longer in our business. If we kept it going just for the money, our lives would become increasingly empty.

In the spring of 2007, our business sold, and I settled into my new position, devoting my full energy to facilitating conversations on the topic of giving. As I did, I began to notice something interesting. At our gatherings the conversations revolved around lofty topics such as leveraged or strategic giving. Those are, of course, excellent things to talk about, but for some reason whenever I told a story of giving from my everyday life, the story resonated with people in a deep way. They would come up to me and say, "I wish I had stories like you have" or "I want the joy that you get from giving."

Something about making giving a part of daily life intrigued people and made them want to try it themselves.

A story I found myself telling a lot was one we like to call "I Like Bike."

A friend had told me there were often leads in the newspaper, so I would regularly scan it for giving opportunities. One Sunday our local paper ran a story about a Sudanese family whose bikes had been stolen. We had planned a family trip to a water park, but I sensed that we should stop and do something about the loss of those bikes immediately. I told Laura and the kids, and they agreed to change our plans. Danny suggested we go buy bikes for them, so we all piled in the van, bought some bikes, and after driving around town for some time, found where the family lived.

No one was home. We waited for a few hours, wondering if this had been a bad idea. Laura kept saying, "Someone else probably gave them bikes already." Doubts began to settle in. We really weren't sure how our unexpected gift would be received.

When the family returned to their house and we approached them to give them the bikes, they were overjoyed! Their English was limited, and all the dad could say was, "I like bike! I like bike!"

As I shared this story with others, I started getting "I Like" stories from all over the country. "I Like Taco Bell," or "I Like Cavities," or "I Like Down Coats." We would text each other whenever something generous happened, and the phrase "I Like" became code for the fact that we had just been able to make someone's day.

A friend of mine, a film producer, picked up on what we were doing and made a short film based on a story we call "I Like Bugshells." We loved it so much that we started making more short films, established a nonprofit organization called I Like Giving, and soon launched our website, ILikeGiving.com. Believing that generosity inspires generosity, we hoped the films and the website would encourage people to create their own "I Like" stories, and it has done just that. What a great privilege to see giving stories coming in from people all around the country and around the world.

●●●

Giving cuts to the very core of what it means to be human. You will read in chapter 5 that new social-scientific research supports the belief that we are created to give. Not only do people report more joy when they give to others, but data indicates that the health benefits of giving are both powerful and long lasting. One study even suggests that giving can dramatically reduce teenage depression and risk of suicide. That's huge.

And that's just the start. From the ancient wisdom passed down through the generations to the most current scientific research, from our own personal experiences to the stories we've been told, what we've learned has convinced us that giving is absolutely essential to life. If you're not experiencing happiness and satisfaction in your life, giving to others could be the one thing that turns that around. Not only does it result in a healthier, happier you, but it creates a better world for all of us.

Because here's the problem: we live in a world that sends us mixed messages. On one hand, we're told to work hard and compete and position ourselves in a fast-moving work environment so we can make as much money as possible and get ahead. On the other hand, we sit in churches or go to fund-raisers where we are asked to be generous. We are bombarded with billboards that tell us we need to be less selfish, that we need to give back or feel guilty about how many people live on less than one dollar a day.

If we're not careful, we find ourselves in a lose-lose situation.

I believe there's another way—a better way.

Living generously is about giving your life to other people so that everything you do—whether it is your work, your charitable giving, or your contribution to your neighborhood—becomes both a gift to others and rewarding for yourself.

This is not a new idea. I am just convinced that it's a really big idea. There are other people all over the world, many I will never meet or hear from, who are living this way—people who wake up every morning with joy and a sense of purpose because they know they are a gift to their communities, their families, their friends, and perhaps the entire world.

That's the type of life we're discovering, and I believe it's how life is meant to be. We also know this type of life is available to anyone, no matter who you are, where you live, or how much money you have. (Giving is about much more than money, after all.)

To enter into the joy of giving, you have to be willing

to go on a journey that will be scary and uncomfortable at times, but it will also be very exhilarating. I know. I've been there. But trust me, if you jump in, you'll never look back. One day you'll wake up and realize you're looking at the world in an entirely different way and you've never felt more alive. When giving opportunities come your way, you'll be ready to embrace them in all their fullness, with all the joy they bring. Giving *is* living, and when you start living generously, you'll be ruined for any other type of life.

Trust me, you'll never look back.

I LIKE
SHARING THE DANCE.

Submitted by: Susan

The father-daughter dance is one of the memorable moments in a wedding, a rite of passage that holds special significance for a daddy and his little girl. While the mother-son dance doesn't always have the heart-tugging impact of the dance with the bride, in my life and the life of my son, Nathan, it became a very emotional moment.

Nathan was only two years old when his father and I went through an unpleasant divorce. It took me years to heal from the hurt of our broken marriage. His dad moved away and married a woman named Eve, who already had a son, Gabriel Michael, eighteen months older than Nathan. This little boy joined Nathan and my other son, Tony, in a new, blended family. Eve and I never developed a relationship; she was simply my sons' stepmom, and we had very few conversations in twenty years.

Nathan's marriage to Holly was a three-day blowout event that created excitement as well as stress. Everyone knew that his dad, Eve, and I were still socially awkward. Despite my stress at having to interact in a close environment, I really wanted Nathan to feel completely relaxed at his wedding.

To enhance their wedding experience, the engaged couple decided to take dance lessons. Big fans of *Dancing with the Stars*, they hoped to look good when they were in the spotlight. Some of us decided to join them, and I began to really look forward to the dance that Nathan and I would share.

The wedding was beautiful—the flowers, the food, and the music. Everything was going as planned, and I was so happy for Nathan and his bride, Holly.

Holly's dance with her father was lovely to watch as they glided effortlessly around the dance floor. Then the emcee called for the groom and his mother to join them, and my moment was finally here. As I took Nathan's hand, our smiles were so huge that I thought our faces would have to expand to hold them. It was so much fun to dance with my grown-up little boy, the child whose heart had been a treasure to me since the day of his birth. And, yes, my eyes began to fill with tears as a flood of happy memories washed over me.

Out of all the people surrounding us, one pair of eyes caught my attention: Eve's. Without knowing where it came from, I suddenly had a desire to share this moment with her. I whispered in Nathan's ear that he should ask Eve to dance. He pulled back slightly, and his face reflected the surprise he felt. "Are you sure?" he asked. I was.

This was not a premeditated change of plans; I believe it was God inspired. Nathan kissed me on the forehead, with tears in his eyes, and danced me to the edge of the

crowd. Then he went over to ask the woman who had been a part of his life for so long to dance the special dance reserved for the mother of the groom.

Watching the two of them dance and struggling to hold back tears, I suddenly remembered why it was so right to encourage them to dance together. Several years before, Eve's only son, Gabriel, was engaged to be married, but he was killed in a car accident. The dance I shared would be the only mother-son dance Eve would ever have.

3
TRY

After many years of interacting with people on the topic of generosity, I have come to believe that most of us do not experience the joy of giving nearly as much as we could. Just thinking about that makes me sad. What if we could change that?

All we have to do is open our eyes and ears to the people around us and then move from awareness to action. If you haven't experienced this type of giving ever or in a long time, today is your day to try.

Doing something generous without anyone telling you to is so exhilarating it becomes addictive. You'll want to do it again. And again.

But if you haven't given in a while, that first time can be hard.

Let me suggest this: Ask for an opportunity to come

your way. Wait for it. And when it comes, seize it. The opportunity might be scary, and you might hesitate and wonder if it's really a good idea after all. Just go with that nudge.

Don't make giving too big a project. Sometimes your best and most perfect gift might be as simple as a smile or a compliment. Maybe it's paying for a stranger's lunch. Maybe it's just passing a bag lunch out the window of a car to a stranger. Maybe it's as simple as sharing a wedding dance.

To be honest, giving opportunities can sometimes catch you off guard or put you in an awkward position. When my family and I sat in front of the Sudanese family's house with those bikes, waiting for someone to come home, I felt a little embarrassed. But if attempting to be generous puts you in a socially awkward position or makes you feel a little uncomfortable, so what? Feeling a little embarrassed is well worth the joy that comes from giving. In fact, your willingness to risk embarrassment can mean a lot to the receiver.

So why not give it a try? Today. Right now. I encourage you to pray the following sentence out loud:

I want to experience the joy that comes from giving. I ask that today an opportunity to give will come my way, that I will recognize it when it does, and that I will have the courage to jump in and give.

Now all you have to do is keep your eyes and ears open as you go about your day and see what happens. I really have no idea what will come your way, but I know this: something *will*. If your eyes are open, if you are available and willing, you will be able to give to someone in a way that will make your day and theirs.

Watch out for these nasty four-letter words: *debt, fear,* and *busy.* They steal joy with the greatest of ease. Be aware of them as they compete with the nudge to do for others.

If an opportunity comes your way and you chicken out, don't beat yourself up about it. When I first started giving this way, I found myself wondering how many people I'd walked past, how many opportunities I'd missed. The good news is that it's never too late to give. If an opportunity comes your way and you don't seize it, don't get stuck in the downward spiral of regret. Smile, tell yourself all is well, and then ask for another one. If there are people around you, there will be more opportunities to give.

It's really as simple as that. It's been said, "Ask and you shall receive." You've asked, and now you will receive. Well, you'll *give*, actually, but sometimes the line between giving and receiving disappears.

You will find that out as you cultivate a lifestyle of giving. What you get back is far greater than anything you give out.

Now you may be scratching your head, wondering what a giving opportunity looks like. Well, there are no limits to what's possible. You just have to use your imagination.

What sparks new ideas for me are stories of people who have given creatively, like these stories from Jeff, Henry, and Billy.

I LIKE MEDICINE: JEFF

Have you ever had one of those moments when, instead of minding your own business as you normally do, you feel compelled to get involved? A few months ago I found myself in a situation like that. I had just finished having lunch with a friend and hopped into my car, fully expecting to continue with my usual day, when the man in the car next to me caught my attention. Even though my window was closed, I could hear his phone conversation and immediately knew he was upset.

Not wanting to eavesdrop but unable to turn a blind eye, I rolled my window down a little bit and listened. He was in a tight spot: his wife had just been to the hospital and needed medicine they could not afford. As he spoke, I could tell that he was not only distressed but really had no idea what to do.

After he got off the phone, I felt moved to talk to him. I rolled down my window and politely told him I had overheard some of his conversation. I asked if he was going to be all right, and he opened up to me, explaining he was unemployed and really had no money at the moment. He was there, in fact, to interview for a job, but right then life was hitting him really hard.

We didn't talk for long because he needed to get to

his interview on time, but as he left, I knew I wanted to help him. There was an ATM nearby, so I drove to it and withdrew a little more than he needed for the medicine. I felt like a secret agent on a mission or something—even his car window helped out by being open a crack. I wrote an encouraging note and slipped it and the twenty-dollar bills through the crack. As I watched them floating down onto his seat, I felt a sense of satisfaction welling up from deep inside.

I'd never seen this man before, and I haven't seen him since. Yet it felt so good to be able to meet his need that day. It was one of those moments when I knew I was meant to help, and there was such a rich joy deep in my soul that came from doing so. Ever since then I have kept an eye out for similar opportunities to give, because even though I'm sure I made his day, helping him really made mine.

●●●

I've told Jeff's story to people so many times, and every time I get the biggest kick out of imagining the twenty-dollar bills floating down onto that man's car seat. All Jeff had to do was keep his eyes open for an opportunity, and sure enough, one came his way. After that it was up to him to take action and seize the day.

Here's another example of seizing a giving opportunity, this time from my friend Henry. His giving story gives new meaning to the phrase *giving the shirt off my back.*

I LIKE GOLF SHIRTS: HENRY

It started out as a regular Saturday afternoon: I was taking my youngest two boys to Chuck E. Cheese's for a birthday party, and their older brother tagged along. I walked in with Graham and Joe, and as I entered the building, the boy manning the entrance rope made a comment about my shirt. "Hey, that's a really, really cool shirt," he said. It was one of my favorites—a very nice University of North Carolina golf shirt. Feeling pretty good about it, I said "thanks" and dropped off the boys at the party.

When I got back to my car, though, the boy's compliment was still with me. Something in the way he had said it—a combination of admiration and longing—made it clear to me he wasn't in a position to afford one of his own anytime soon. Without thinking through the consequences too much, I whipped off my shirt and sent my oldest son to give it to him.

Driving home shirtless, I found myself picturing the looks on my neighbors' faces when I got home. Fred would almost certainly be mowing the lawn, as he always did on a Saturday afternoon. What would he think when I got out of my van in only my jeans and sandals? I hoped I wasn't making a fool of myself for no good reason. When I got home, the dash from my van to my house really wasn't all that bad, and the truth is that I loved giving my shirt away. The best part about it for me was that I felt sure the boy at Chuck E. Cheese's loved receiving a shirt he never expected to have.

●●●

What Henry experienced that day is something that some of us call "the nudge"—a sense that you want to give something to someone even though you're not completely sure why. Your heart beats a little faster, and you get a little nervous, and you might even tell yourself it's a bad idea, but you know it's something you're meant to do. Henry followed that nudge, and because he did, he not only made someone else's day, but now he has a funny story to tell.

I LIKE FLAG LADY: BILLY

My wife and I were driving from Springfield, Illinois, back home to Kentucky and decided to take a shortcut. Highway 4 is a heavily traveled two-lane road between two major highways. Usually it saves the time it takes to drive all the way through St. Louis. That day the shortcut wasn't so short—but it sure was sweet.

It was a hot, uncomfortable day in the middle of summer. Road construction had shut everything down to one lane, and cars were backed up for miles on both sides. Tempers were flaring in front of us and behind us, and the rising temperatures didn't help a lick. After waiting nearly forty-five minutes, my wife and I pulled up to the flag lady—the lucky construction worker in charge of keeping all these ornery drivers at bay.

That's when I rolled down the window, letting in a stream of humid summer air.

"How you doin' ma'am?" I asked politely. The flag lady responded with a wipe of her wrinkled brow and the thickest country accent I'd ever heard.

"Honey, I'm doin' fine! You been waitin' a long time?"

"Why, ma'am, it ain't too bad," I said, trying to be friendly.

"Well, I'm glad you the one pulled up here," she said, exasperated. "They've been people pullin' up here cussing me, flippin' me off, and I can't do anything but my job!"

"Ma'am, you know what? You're doing a great job," I said. "What's your name?"

"Honey, my name is Crazy Cathy," she said. "Everybody calls me that!"

"Well, Cathy, it's nice to meet you." I laughed. "I'm Billy Moore. Cathy, do you live around here?"

"Oh yeah!" she exclaimed. "I live around here. My kids live with me; my grandkids live with me."

I learned a lot about Cathy over the next few minutes, and all the while my wife listened patiently to the conversation. I couldn't imagine being a hardworking grandmother with kids and grandkids living at home, out here on the hottest days, holding signs and waving flags. With my right hand I signaled with a rub of my thumb against two fingers for my wife to get out a little money. Cathy didn't notice, but my wife handed me a twenty-dollar bill.

"Well, honey, looks like it's about time for me to let you come through here!" Cathy said brightly. "Hope you have a good day!"

I said, "Cathy, I hope you have a great day! And I have something the Lord wants me to give you." I reached my hand out the window and handed Cathy the twenty-dollar bill.

I was not prepared for what happened next.

First, Cathy dropped her Stop sign. Then she jumped up on the running board of our truck, leaned in, put both arms around me, and planted a kiss right on my lips.

Then she jumped back, grabbed her pole, and flipped on her walkie-talkie.

"Alex!" she shouted into the speaker. "You be nice to this guy in the white truck coming through. We're eating pizza tonight because of him."

As we rolled through the construction zone, I stared out the windshield, still in shock. My wife broke the silence with a line we won't soon forget.

"Honey," she said laughing, "I never thought I would enjoy seeing another woman kiss you."

●●●

How hilarious is that? Can you just picture Cathy the flag lady jumping up on Billy's truck and kissing him on the lips? Imagine if Billy had approached his situation differently. What if being stuck in traffic had soured him to the point of not being aware of the opportunity standing right next to him? If you keep a positive attitude and look for ways to give, it can really make your day.

Waking up that morning, Jeff, Henry, and Billy never thought they'd do what they did that day. Yet when a giving opportunity intersected their lives, they were aware enough to act on it. Lives were changed—the lives of people they gave to and their own. In a small way they changed their world.

This life requires a little creativity, open eyes, and a personal touch. It isn't hard, but it won't happen if you don't try.

So give it a try.

Once you've gone out and found your own I Like Giving opportunity, I encourage you to share it. Tweet about it, put it as your Facebook status, call a friend, or tell your dog about it. Just share it however your heart desires. And remember that your motive matters. This is about encouraging and inspiring others—not about bragging or having your name in lights.

For those of you who enjoy writing, I have included a place for you to write your giving story at the end of this book. Don't worry if you're no Shakespeare. Writing your story isn't about impressing anyone with your literary skills. Just write it down for yourself so you'll have a record of your story. It's a great way to look back on what happened, and then you'll have a record of it to read in the future or to share with friends and family.

If you're feeling brave, you could even send it to us at ILikeGiving.com, and we'll share it with the world. We'd love to hear your story!

I LIKE COFFEE AND PINK LIPSTICK.

Submitted by: Brad

Even on a hot summer day in Florida, a good Starbucks coffee hits the spot. I pulled over and headed to my favorite caffeine oasis, ready to quench my need for coffee and then hit the beach. Once inside I realized I was not alone in my choice—the place was humming.

One Starbucks patron in particular caught my eye. I still don't know her name, but she must have been about eighty-five years old. Everything about her was pink. I mean, she was wearing pink shoes, a pink hat, pink nail polish, and pink lipstick. Even her cheeks had some pink makeup on them.

When the lady in pink joined the line behind me, a thought popped into my mind: *I'm going to buy her coffee.* Immediately I felt the excitement of being on an undercover giving mission. When I got to the front, I used my height to block Pink Lipstick Lady's view of the barista and told him my plan. "The older woman in line behind me—the one with the pink hat—I want to pay for her coffee," I said.

Realizing he could be in on a stealth mission, the barista grinned and agreed to make it happen.

I stepped aside and listened as the lady in pink placed her order. "I would like a grande eleven-pump vanilla latte, please."

The barista was surprised. "Whoa! That's usually a three-pump drink."

"Starbucks has it all wrong," she cheerfully explained. "You should tell these Starbucks people it is eleven pumps. I've tried six. I've tried seven. I've tried nine pumps of vanilla. Eleven is the best."

"Not ten?" he asked.

"Oh, no, no! Not ten. It must be exactly eleven pumps!"

My coffee was ready and waiting. I reached for it and headed to the door. As I did, I overheard the barista say to the lady in pink, "Your coffee is taken care of, ma'am. That gentleman over there paid for it."

She slowly turned toward me. "Who are you?" Her voice, as light as a summer breeze, carried across the room. She snapped her pink purse closed as she walked directly toward me—right when I thought I had gotten away.

I shrugged. "I'm just a guy from Michigan."

"Did you just win the lottery?"

"No," I answered. "I just wanted to do something nice."

Appreciation blossomed across her face. "You have just changed my view of humanity!" she exclaimed. "I'm going to tell all my kids up in Canada. I've never had anybody do this for me before. I am just astounded by what you did today!"

An amazing smile spread across her face. I left, but that face will always be etched in my mind—pink lipsticked lips stretched into the biggest smile you can imagine.

I'll never forget buying an eleven-shot vanilla latte for the lady in pink.

4

WHAT HAPPENS WHEN WE GIVE

Giving can be a wild ride. One minute you're standing in a public place, minding your own business. The next you're approaching a stranger with a slightly awkward smile trying to explain that you'd like to give something to him or her. Maybe your personal giving experiences haven't led you into uncharted territory yet, but if you stick with it, they will.

Giving can also get messy. Sometimes we give to people who don't respond the way we hoped they would. Sometimes it just doesn't seem to work out. I remember being disappointed at times early in my giving experiences. I would give, and the receiver wouldn't seem grateful. Sometimes it seemed like the receiver didn't even notice. Other times I was flat-out rejected or was met with such an emotional response that I wasn't quite sure what to do with myself.

The key in all these situations is to remember that giving to others is not only about how the receivers respond. Sometimes we need to give more than other people need to receive. Sometimes we are so wrapped up in our own little worlds of self-focused living that, even in giving, we can get caught up focusing on ourselves. Living in that self-centered head space is miserable. Thankfully, there is a solution that works every time: give with no strings attached.

Early in my journey, I found myself getting hung up on being thanked in a certain way or noticed for my generosity. Over time I realized that my expectation of a "right" response made the whole thing less of a gift and more of a transaction. When I allowed myself to find joy in giving regardless of the receiver's response, I found I could enjoy giving every time.

Giving repeatedly shifted my perspective away from me and toward other people. As that happened, my expectations of how my giving should be received faded. The more I focus on helping others, the less I focus on me, and that makes my heart come alive.

When you give, you may not be around to see how the receiver responds. If you're ever left wondering whether your gift was appreciated, a little story I call "I Like Laundry" will give you a good idea.

I LIKE LAUNDRY: CARLIE

If there's anything I hate, it's laundry. Sitting around in my dorm room all day, waiting for clothes to wash and dry, then painstakingly folding each piece? No thank you. I'm a busy college student with papers to write, classes to attend, and studying to do. To me, wasting hours on laundry is the highest form of cruel and unusual punishment. So as a freshman in college, I came up with a strategy to deal with my least favorite chore: I didn't do it.

Two months went by without a trip downstairs to my dorm's laundry room—that smelly dungeon where you have to pay a dollar per load to watch your life pass by. In a matter of eight weeks, I wore every pair of underwear, worked through my entire wardrobe, and accumulated a pile of dirty clothes so high you'd have thought I was trying for a world record.

What I was trying was my roommate's patience.

One day she kindly mentioned that my dirty clothes bin (which was conspicuously overflowing onto our floor) needed some attention. I wasn't happy to hear the motherly concern in her voice, but she was right. I'd officially run out of clean clothes.

That day I grudgingly filled my laundry basket full of soured T-shirts, shorts, jeans, and towels and headed to that most dreaded place: the laundry room. There I stuffed one washer full to the brim with every last item and a capful of soap. Quickly I paid my dollar, turned the knob, and headed to class.

The next morning I woke up in sheer terror. There I was in pajamas, late for class—without a single thing to wear.

How had I been so careless? After my brave journey to the laundry cave, I'd left my clothes in the washer and never returned. Everything I owned was down there. At best my clothes would be mildewed in the washer. But what was more likely was that they'd been stolen by some other co-ed who thought it was her lucky day!

In a panic I rushed downstairs into the laundry room and threw open every washer door. Empty, empty, empty.

And then it happened. Looking around, I noticed something on top of one of the dryers: three evenly spaced laundry bags filled to the brim with perfectly folded shirts and pants as if they'd been pressed professionally. *If only I could be that responsible,* I thought, *then I wouldn't have to go out and buy a whole new wardrobe!* How would I explain this to my parents?

On the verge of tears, I scoured every corner of the room, looking for a spare sock or an abandoned tank top, hoping desperately for a clue.

I looked again at that stack of perfectly laundered clothes and peeked inside one of the bags. The clothes were mine. There was a small card stapled to the front of one of the bags. It read:

> *Carlie,*
> *I thought you may be needing these.*
> *Just wanted to help you a little bit during*
> *this stressful time.*
> *xoxo*

Some basement angel had paid for my laundry to dry, folded each and every garment, bagged it all beautifully, and left it for me to find. As I stood there in the laundry room, I couldn't believe the kindness of this anonymous stranger. I was amazed at how a small act of service meant so much to me.

That moment changed me.

Don't get me wrong. I still hate laundry. But now, every time I trudge downstairs with my big bin of dirty clothes, I smile and remember the power of that act of service. Now laundry reminds me that I don't have to spend millions to be generous—even completing one small chore might be all it takes to save the day.

● ● ●

Something as basic as folding someone else's laundry without being asked can change that person's day and communicate a sense of kindness that sticks for years. How worthwhile is that?

Chuck, a friend of mine, shared with me a story that involved his brother-in-law. It's especially fun because brother-in-law relationships can be quirky at times. As you'll see, the gift was very much appreciated even though it took a few months for it to be acknowledged.

I LIKE FLOOR MATS: CHUCK

It is hard to characterize my brother-in-law, James. He's not a guy who draws a lot of attention to himself, and he's not a guy with great wealth. In fact, James is, well, quite average, but when it comes to generosity, James is one of the most above-average people I've ever met.

For instance, if James needed to borrow your car, he would likely return it with a full tank of fuel or maybe a new set of tires. Or maybe it would have been detailed. And unless you happened to notice, he wouldn't draw any attention to it.

Which is exactly what happened with the floor mats in our Honda Accord. They were worn-out. I mean, they're floor mats. They are one of those things you think about replacing when you vacuum the car and say to yourself, "Wow, these look terrible. I need to replace them." You finish vacuuming, put the mats back, and never give them another thought until the next time you clean your car.

However, this particular time I *did* notice them. They were new. I immediately asked my wife if she'd bought the new car mats. She said she thought I had. Immediately we knew it was James. I could not think of when he might have done it. I went back in the house, called him, and asked if he was responsible. As I suspected, he was.

"When did you put new mats in the car?" I asked since we hadn't seen him in weeks.

"About three months ago," he sheepishly replied.

I couldn't believe I'd been so unobservant, but I wasn't the least bit surprised by James's thoughtful act of generosity. It's a lifestyle with him. I truly can't think of anything he enjoys doing more than giving, and I can't think of anyone who has more fun finding unique ways to give. I mean, who would ever think of replacing someone's floor mats?

●●●

James was happy to give without being acknowledged. Three months went by, and he didn't say a word. He just enjoyed knowing that he had given to Chuck even if Chuck never found out. For James, the reward was simply the joy of knowing he had blessed someone else, whether that person realized it or not.

I LIKE NOT BEING REJECTED: JOY

I have a dear friend named Anne, who knows me better than just about anyone. She's blond and petite, and when she rolls her eyes, she cracks me up every single time. Through the years we've laughed and cried over some of life's best and worst experiences. We met our husbands the same year. We got married the same year. I had a baby; then she had a baby. When I was diagnosed with cancer, sadly, Anne was diagnosed with cancer too.

When Anne pulled through her final surgery, a crazy idea came to my mind. What if she and I went on a cruise together? We'd both been through so much pain, uncertainty, and fear. Wouldn't a jaunt through the Caribbean be the perfect recipe for recovery?

There was only one problem. Anne's husband was unemployed, and I was certain they couldn't afford such an extravagant trip. When I mentioned the idea to my husband, he astonished me with his response. So many people had showered us with kindness during our battle with cancer. Why not bless Anne with a free ticket?

I couldn't contain my excitement! I imagined boarding the cruise ship with her, sunglasses on and bags packed, and then heading out for a week on the open seas. I could almost taste the salty air on my tongue and feel the golden sun on my back. With tears of joy in my eyes, I picked up the phone.

I remember the excitement in Anne's voice and her heartfelt gratitude. Then she paused and said that before we bought the tickets, she'd need to talk with her husband.

A few days went by before I heard from her, and this time the excitement was drained from her voice. She said the cruise wasn't going to happen. Then she said, "Please, let's not talk about this again."

I was devastated. With just a few words, my closest friend shut down the biggest act of generosity I'd ever attempted. I felt as if I'd been punched in the gut. Was there something wrong with my gift? Or worse, was something wrong with me? Or was it her husband's pride?

We haven't brought it up again, and to this day the rejection stings like an old burn that's still tender. I don't know exactly what happened, but I have a theory: perhaps when we are in need, the hardest thing to do is to have those needs met by someone else.

How I wish she had said yes.

● ● ●

That's hard to read. I don't know what your experience has been, but for me few things are more hurtful than offering a generous gift and having it rejected, especially by a close friend.

Understand that, for many, receiving can be hard.

If something similar happens to you, don't stop giving. If your generosity is rejected, understand that it's the other person's issue, not yours. Keep practicing generosity, even if it's not received as you had hoped.

As Dr. Kent Keith famously wrote, "People are illogical, unreasonable, and self-centered. Love them anyway. If you do good, people will accuse you of selfish ulterior motives. Do good anyway…. The good you do today will be forgotten tomorrow. Do good anyway…. Give the world the best you have and you'll get kicked in the teeth. Give the world the best you have anyway."[1]

I LIKE TURBULENCE.

Submitted by: Bill

I enjoy flying. While some people find boarding a plane and traveling through the sky a frightening experience, I've always thought of it as an adventure. My dad was an air force pilot, so you could say it's in my blood.

One particular morning I was on a flight out of Chicago on a small commuter jet. With wind and rain outside, I guessed we might be heading into some rough weather. It was only a short hop over Lake Michigan—no more than an hour—but small planes are notoriously bad in stormy weather, and I feared we were in for a bumpy ride.

About ten minutes into the flight, my suspicions were proved correct. We hit massive turbulence, and the plane bumped around like a bull rider on a bad day. With our seat belts buckled and our tray tables up, we were making the best of it, but it was rough.

After a few minutes I realized there was a sound coming from behind me. I hadn't noticed it before because of the noise of the plane, but I realized that the lady sitting behind me was saying something. I couldn't distinguish the words at first, but then it hit me—she was praying!

Without thinking about it, I knew I wanted to help her

somehow. I bent my arm up and around and stuck my hand back through the gap between the side of the plane and my seat. I'd never met this lady, and I couldn't even see her, but we were in this storm together, and she needed a hand.

I honestly didn't know what her reaction would be to this strange hand coming from the seat in front of her, but she immediately latched on to it with all her might!

The storm continued for the next forty-five minutes. For the entire time we held hands. We probably looked a bit strange, and I was definitely in a contorted, awkward position, but we didn't care. We just held on and rode out the storm together.

Finally the wheels came down, and we were settled on solid ground. Only then did she let go.

As we stood to deplane, I turned around and for the first time saw the lady whose hand I had held through the storm. She smiled at me, and I knew what it meant. It meant "thank you," and I could see the sincere gratitude on her face.

In the world we live in, we can often feel isolated, but in moments like these, we can feel a connection to someone who would otherwise be a complete stranger. If I hadn't extended my hand to the lady behind me, that flight would have been just another bumpy ride. Because I did, it is a flight I will never forget.

5
THE SCIENCE OF GIVING

By now you've read a lot of stories, including my own, about the joy of generosity. Hopefully you've also given it a try and have shared your own experience of giving. I love stories, and I love experiences, but sometimes I need a little more. Recently published scientific studies affirm what I already believed—that it's more satisfying to give than to receive. These studies suggest that giving to others not only makes us happier but can make us healthier as well. I think you'll be encouraged by just how extensive the science of giving really is.

MONEY CAN BUY HAPPINESS: THE SURPRISING COUNTERINTUITIVE FINDINGS OF ELIZABETH DUNN AND MICHAEL NORTON

Elizabeth Dunn is a social psychologist and associate

professor at the University of British Columbia, Vancouver, Canada. Michael Norton is an associate professor of business administration at the Harvard Business School in Boston, Massachusetts. Together they published the fascinating book *Happy Money: The Science of Smarter Spending*.[2] (In November 2011, Norton also presented some of his findings at a TEDx event held in Cambridge, Massachusetts.)

Dunn, Norton, and their team asked the question, "What if money *can* buy us happiness if we spend it in a different way?" Specifically, the authors wanted to know if spending money on others, instead of on ourselves, could make us happier. Their research confirmed what we've already been experiencing at I Like Giving: while spending money on ourselves doesn't improve our happiness all that much, spending money on others does.

Dunn and Norton surveyed Americans, asking them about their happiness and their spending habits. What they found was that "prosocial spending" was linked to higher levels of happiness (*prosocial spending* means spending money on others or donating money to charity). Continuing their research, Dunn and Norton conducted a more detailed examination of workers who spent their profit-sharing bonuses in different ways. The only factor that consistently showed correlation between spending and happiness was, again, prosocial spending. The more people spent money on others or gave it away, the happier they reported being.

Wanting to make sure this conclusion applied to a

random sampling of people on the street, Dunn and Norton conducted a survey of students at the University of British Columbia. Students were first asked questions about how happy they were. Then they were given an amount of money with instructions to spend it either on themselves or on someone else by five o'clock that evening. When the research team called the students that night, the prosocial spenders reported feeling happier. The self-focused spenders reported no significant difference. Interestingly, the amount was not a major factor—whether people spent five dollars or twenty, the act of spending money on someone else brought a significant boost in happiness.

Now, I know what you're wondering—*Does this apply only to relatively wealthy people in North America?* Well, Dunn and Norton asked that question too. To find the answer, they conducted a similar study in Uganda, one of the world's poorest countries, and found similar results: when people spent money on other people, they felt happier. When they spent money on themselves, it didn't really affect their happiness at all. The authors note that the specific way in which you spend on other people isn't nearly as important as the fact that you simply do it.

And their research didn't end there. Their team contacted Gallup, the polling and survey organization. Gallup surveyed people across the globe, asking them questions about charitable giving and general happiness. When the results came in, they confirmed the research the team had already done: in almost every country around the world, a positive correlation exists between giving and happiness!

Through their research Dunn and Norton confirmed that spending money on other people is powerfully life giving. It's as if we're created to give. Giving satisfies our most essential self, increases our happiness, and makes us feel more alive.

THE GOOD LIFE: A STUDY OF EXTRINSIC VERSUS INTRINSIC GOALS

A friend recently recommended the book *Drive: The Surprising Truth About What Motivates Us* by Daniel H. Pink.[3] It's a fascinating look at what really motivates people and how the workplace is adjusting to twenty-first-century expectations. What stood out to me in the book was the research Pink included about giving. In his section on purpose, he highlights a study by several professors at the University of Rochester in New York. Their findings point to the satisfaction that comes from giving your life away.

The professors contacted college students who were about to graduate. The students agreed to answer questions about their goals one year after graduation and again one year later. Goals that related to helping others were categorized as "intrinsic aspirations"; goals related to money or recognition were labeled "extrinsic goals." What the professors found was that, essentially, students who had intrinsic goals—goals that had to do with helping others or making a positive contribution to the world—and met their goals reported an increase in satisfaction and well-being. Students who had extrinsic goals, however, even if they achieved high levels of success, reported no significant increase in life satisfaction. In fact, graduates with profit-focused goals actually reported higher levels of anxiety, depression, and other negative emotions. The researchers point out that, in these cases, the achievement of self-centered goals actually made the graduates' lives worse.

That's remarkable. The bottom line of their research is that, no matter how successful you are, it is giving your life away to others that makes you happy. I think we've all heard stories about people who work hard all their lives only to find that the success they dreamed about didn't give them what they hoped it would. The right response, though, is not to shun success but to replace selfish ambition with other ambitions—doing things for others. That is the type of ambition that brings you life and makes the world a better place.

WHY GOOD THINGS HAPPEN TO GOOD PEOPLE: THE INCREDIBLE FINDINGS OF STEPHEN POST

Did you know that giving actually has measurable health benefits and can help you live longer? These are just some of the findings by my friend Dr. Stephen Post.

Post, who is director of the Center for Medical Human-ities, Compassionate Care, and Bioethics at Stony Brook

University in New York, has spent most of his life in the world of bioethics. In 2001, with the help of a generous grant from the John Templeton Foundation, he founded the Institute for Research on Unlimited Love.

What Dr. Post has scientifically proven is nothing short of remarkable. By funding more than fifty studies at forty-four major universities, IRUL has accumulated staggering data to suggest that giving does more than make us happy. It makes us *healthier*. Dr. Post says the following in the opening of *Why Good Things Happen to Good People,* the book he coauthored with Jill Neimark: "I have one simple message to offer and it's this: giving is the most potent force on the planet."[4] He goes on to write, "Give daily, in small ways, and you will be happier. Give and you will be healthier. Give, and you will even live longer."[5]

He even makes the claim that "giving protects over-all health twice as much as aspirin protects against heart disease."[6]

One of the studies that IRUL inherited began in the 1920s at the University of California at Berkley. The study spanned more than sixty years and provided striking data that helping others results in long-term health benefits. Remember the research that showed giving reduces depression and the risk of suicide for teenagers? That research is also from Dr. Post.

What I really appreciate about Post is that he doesn't put giving only in the box of money or things. While Elizabeth Dunn and Michael Norton studied the effects of giving money to other people, Stephen Post focused on nonmonetary giving. He defined ten ways of giving: celebration, "generativity" (helping others grow), forgiveness, courage, humor, respect, compassion, loyalty, listening, and creativity. Each of these is a way to give to others and to ourselves, and together they cover a vast range of the ways we interact with the world.

Why Good Things Happen to Good People also suggests four main areas in which we can do our giving: family, friends, community, and humanity. The message of the book is that if we learn to live our lives as a gift to those around us, near or far, in the unique ways we are best at, we will be happier, healthier, and will live longer simply through giving.

I'm not a scientist, but I find studies like these inspiring. They echo the words of renowned author Henri Nouwen, who said, "Every time I take a step in the direction of generosity, I know that I am moving from fear to love."[7]

Giving is a powerful force. The research proves it. Giving gives us life. It connects us to other people, brings us joy, and increases our well-being.

I LIKE
PAY PHONES.

Submitted by: Robert

Plenty of people view traveling as their personal time to be in a horrid mood. Grumbling and sighing are the soundtrack of a security checkpoint full of barefoot, befuddled professionals with multiple chips on well-dressed shoulders.

But I look forward to traveling with a different perspective.

Rather than complaining through security, I embrace removing my shoes, unpacking a perfectly organized briefcase, and raising my arms in submission. After all, on the other side of that security checkpoint in the Atlanta airport lies my favorite airport reward: a spicy chicken Chick-fil-A sandwich.

One day I was already dreaming of that first crispy, well-seasoned bite when I noticed a stout woman in a dark gray wool jacket wobbling toward me. She held a carry-on bag, and her graying hair was pinned back expertly, exposing a wrinkled face and a worried expression. Before I knew it, she was standing directly in front of me, asking if I knew where to find a pay phone. Her accent was gruff and consonant filled—German.

I was speechless for a moment, wondering when I'd last *actually seen* a pay phone. Then I pulled my cell phone from my back pocket and held it toward her. "Here's your pay phone," I said.

The woman handed me her purse and rolling bag and walked away, cradling my phone in both hands.

There in the middle of the concourse, I stood incredulous, watching this woman walk away with my phone, leaving me alone with her luggage, which by now I was quite certain contained explosives. Almost on cue the automated message echoed above, reminding travelers to alert authorities if someone they didn't know had given them his or her belongings. I fidgeted nervously. Who was this woman? What had I just done?

I could see her thirty yards away, gesturing to an attendant at a gate, then speaking into my phone intently. A few moments later she marched back in my direction. She gently placed the phone back in my hand and clasped her other hand on the bottom, sandwiching my phone and hand in a warm squeeze. "You're an angel," she said with sincerity.

At this point I was ready to nod my head and make a beeline for my spicy chicken sandwich, but she stopped me once more. This time she didn't ask for a pay phone. Instead, she asked if she could pray for me.

Swallowing my hunger, I realized we were sharing something special in the middle of concourse A. Around us, bustling travelers on their way to their gates about knocked us over. Rather than let the hassles and inconveniences of travel distract me, I'd had my own adventure right there.

She laid her wrinkled hands on my arms and spoke words of thanks to God for the angel with the phone.

That day, the wait for my spicy chicken sandwich was well worth it.

6
GIVING FILTERS

Giving to others is an amazing, life-giving, joy-increasing thing to do. Yet sometimes we hold back from giving for a variety of reasons. I have realized at times that I have established filters in my thinking when it comes to giving—biases that obstruct my willingness to give.

Here are some of the giving filters I've had to knock down over the years:

"They'll just waste it if I give to them."

"I shouldn't give unless I get a tax deduction."

"This isn't a good time."

"I'm comfortable, and giving will make me uncomfortable."

"They don't really need it."

Filters like these are created by past experiences and thought patterns, ways of thinking that lead to assumptions that are not necessarily true. Honestly, I think I have filters when it comes to all sorts of things, but giving has definitely been a very filtered area for me.

Have you ever stopped to think why you see things the way you do? My thinking about giving was so influenced by building campaigns, white envelopes, and charity fund-raiser dinners that I developed a resistance toward giving. These experiences caused me to think about giving as an obligation. Yes, I had grown up with my grandpa as an example, but other negative associations about giving crept in over the years. With so many filters in place, I was being robbed of the full joy of a generous life. Don't get me wrong. I love giving to my local church and other non-profits, but I don't do it out of a sense of duty. I do it because I've purposed in my heart. It's now my idea.

Of course it is good to be wise in our giving. There might be good reasons to hold back from giving a gift. At the same time, we want to be sure that filters don't rob us of life-giving opportunities to give.

The truth is that none of us can fully see the big picture; sometimes what we think makes sense just doesn't. There have been times I felt the nudge to give to someone even though it made no rational sense. I gave anyway. Learning to be sensitive to your spirit, to "listen to the situation," and to make gut-based decisions can give you a useful set of tools in your giving journey. Sometimes the giving that makes the least amount of sense brings the most joy.

In the past I had always looked at giving from a needs-based perspective. I now have a broader perspective on giving that includes being a blessing to others who may not have a perceived need.

When I tell giving stories, some people immediately assume I'm talking about giving money to a man on the street with a cardboard sign. Talk about a subject that brings up filters! I hope you realize that this type of giving is not the essence of what this book is about. We are championing a lifestyle of generosity, whether to strangers or family, whether with money or a smile.

That said, most of us encounter the man-on-the-street situation from time to time. So how do we respond to it? Especially in First World countries, including the United States, it can be hard to trust someone on the street who is begging for money; our filter reminds us, "They'll only use the money I give them for drugs or alcohol." This may be a legitimate concern, but I want to caution you—don't let the occasional person who abuses the goodwill of others ruin your giving and deter you.

As a general rule, when I see someone asking for money on the street, I look for that nudge in my spirit to give. In most cases people in situations like that would benefit more from sustained help than a one-time monetary gift. Even so, if I feel the nudge, I will readily hand over some cash. What they do with the money is their decision; my choice is whether to harden my heart toward them or to allow myself to feel compassion. Compassion doesn't mean giving every time, but when I give, I do it knowing that I've loved a fellow human being right where that person is, whether the money will be wasted or not.

Another approach is to give something besides money. One friend of mine will pack bag lunches and keep them in his car for people on the street. Other people will give the gift of time, stopping to talk and listen to the person's story. I've done that before, and it was both meaningful and rewarding. We can never know for sure why someone is asking for money, so brush off any offense or sense of obligation, and if you feel compelled, give. I find myself being grateful I'm not in that situation.

Sometimes when I get hung up on these types of issues, I really have to stop and laugh at myself. Seriously, how many times have I wasted money? I'm not fueling an addiction with my income, but I can't say I always spend my money wisely. Can you? Why should I condemn people who do the same thing? When you give with the right heart, you release the receivers to use your gift in any way they choose.

Another thought: sometimes just acknowledging other people is enough to help them turn their lives around. Your trust in giving them something can be a catalyst for hope. What you actually give sometimes means less than the fact you stopped and cared. That was the case in the following story.

I LIKE STRAWBERRY MILKSHAKES: FRANCIS
I was stepping out of a store in Birmingham, Alabama, on

a cold December day when a lady behind me said, "Hey! I'm hungry." I turned around as she repeated herself, a little louder this time. She was elderly, her clothes were ragged, and she held an old bag in her lap.

"Do you have some change? I'm hungry," she said.

I apologized that I didn't have any cash on me and continued on my way. As I approached my car, however, I saw a Burger King on the other side of the parking lot and decided I could help her after all. Pulling my car around to where she was sitting, I asked if she would like something from the King.

"A strawberry milkshake!" she replied.

A milkshake. Seriously? It must have been thirty degrees outside, and she wanted a milkshake? I checked to make sure, but she insisted that a milkshake was what she wanted. I told her I'd get her a hamburger and some fries too.

Returning from the drive-through, I gave her the burgers, fries, and, yes, the strawberry milkshake. She looked up at me and said, "Most of the time people just see me and keep walking like I don't even exist. Thank you for acknowledging me."

How many times have I passed someone in need and kept walking? How many times have I not only refused to help but not even acknowledged the person's need? In that moment of seeing her gratitude, it really hit me—what mattered to her more than the milkshake and the food was simply that I took the time to see her and care.

●●●

At I Like Giving, we sometimes call that story "I Like Being Acknowledged" because being seen meant more to the lady in the story than the milkshake or the food. Sometimes when people are down-and-out or in a hard life situation, simply letting them know that other people see them and care about them is the most important thing we can do. If you give money to people who live on the street, they may waste it, but the fact that you stopped to acknowledge them may be all that is needed for them to turn their lives around.

My hope is that you will sense the abundant life that comes from giving to another person, regardless of whether your gift makes total sense or how the receiver uses what is given. When you give to others and they seem to waste it, it's discouraging, but loving someone else never goes to waste. Of course, if you feel your generosity is being abused or wasted, then it is good and right to reevaluate. If it is a stranger, then continue on your way. If it is a family member or someone in your community, give the gift of forgiveness and allow it to inform your wisdom for future giving, but don't stop giving. Don't let one or two bad experiences rob you of the joy.

I LIKE HEAD LICE: MICHAEL

I'm a bottom-line type of guy.

If I see a problem that needs fixing and I can do

something about it, I do it. So when one of the girls in my fifth-grade class was in danger of falling behind because of a case of head lice, I stepped in.

I'd been teaching at a Christian school in a fairly affluent part of town for several years before Katie showed up in my class. Katie's parents were going through a bitter divorce, and we all knew they were having trouble at home. Katie was often late to school, unkempt, and behind on her homework. We all hoped her home life wouldn't totally destroy her studies, so I looked out for her however I could. Things got worse, however, when she showed up at school with head lice. The administration had to send her home until she was no longer contagious.

For the next two weeks, I looked on as a cycle developed: Katie's mom would claim the lice were gone, and Katie would show up at school and then be sent home because they were still there. Now, as you might know, someone having lice makes a good number of people uncomfortable. For Katie, though, the stakes were a lot higher. If someone didn't jump in and take the bull by the horns, this might go on indefinitely, and she wouldn't finish the fifth grade.

The solution was obvious. I called my wife. "Honey," I said, "I have a girl in my class who has head lice. I want to bring her home and take care of them. She might need to stay with us for a few days. Do you think that would be okay?" Of course my wife and I were concerned that the lice might spread to ourselves or our three children, but we agreed it was the best thing to do. If we were careful, it should be fine.

After getting permission from Katie's mom, we brought her to our house and began the crusade to cure her infested hair.

I spread out a big tarp on the floor and sat Katie down on a chair in front of our television. I had acquired an arsenal of antilice paraphernalia and was determined to leave no louse standing. Katie's hair was long and practically exploding with the little critters, but this was war. I wasn't about to back down.

Four hours later I had deloused Katie well and good, I thought, and we all went to bed expecting her to be back in school in the morning.

But the next day the school took one look at Katie's hair and declared that some of the ever-persistent lice had survived. The trouble was that Katie's hair was just so thick and long that I hadn't been able to tell whether the battle had been won. We took her to get her hair cut and told the stylist to cut it short. Several pounds of hair later, the situation was more manageable.

This time our efforts to eradicate the pestilence were successful.

Katie's parents were grateful for our help. They allowed her to stay with us for a few weeks while she caught up at school. I made arrangements for their home to be fumigated so the lice would not return. Even though I had tried to keep things quiet, several other parents heard about Katie's situation and took the initiative to get her some new lice-free clothes.

Having her in the house was not easy, as she was not accustomed to a disciplined home environment, but for the reward of helping her, it was worth it. Katie continued to attend school lice-free, didn't miss another day, and had a great year.

I'm forty-one now. If you'd asked me when I was thirty-one what life was all about, I probably would have said something about making money and getting ahead. I don't think like that anymore. Jesus said that it is better to give than to receive, and I now know that's the truth. Climbing the corporate ladder or trying to prove to others that I am a success doesn't mean anything to me anymore.

Right now I don't have the means to be enormously generous with my finances, but I do what I can, mostly with my time. I've changed jobs and now work with at-risk inner-city kids during the day. I look for ways to live my life as a gift to others however I can. The reward of giving, even if it takes putting yourself in an uncomfortable situation, is so lasting and satisfying that, when I think back to the time I helped Katie, I'm thankful for the gift that experience was to me.

● ● ●

Now that's the gift of inconvenience. Most of the parents at that school were so scared their children might get lice from Katie that they wouldn't let them anywhere near her. Yet Michael took her into his own home and persevered until the lice were gone. It was inconvenient and messy, but it was worth it and made a difference in both of their lives.

I LIKE VANS: BRAD

I met William at a Bible study one morning and liked him right away. He and his family had just moved from Nigeria. A few months later he mentioned he really wanted to go to a local jail to encourage the inmates with his story. The biggest problem was that he didn't have transportation.

I found out he was working as a janitor at a museum, trying to save enough to buy a used van. He never asked for anything, but I felt a nudge to help him out. I called a friend who owns a car dealership. He said, "Great, I want in on that." I wasn't asking him to help, but he insisted: "I really want to do this kind of giving but don't know how to find the opportunities."

We teamed up to find the right van and came across a green Chrysler minivan that was big enough to hold William's family of eight. We went ahead and got car insurance too so they would be ready to go. William's family got a ride to the dealership to pick up the van. They were all so excited as they ran up to it—especially the six kids.

A few months later I ran into William at a church meeting. I asked if he'd been able to get to the jail yet.

"Well, there's a little bit of a problem," he replied.

I'm thinking, *Oh no. A wreck?* What was the problem?

"I don't have a driver's license," he said.

I didn't see that one coming!

"Yeah, I keep going to this place where they charge me $80 to take the test, and I keep failing it," he said. He'd been saving his ten-dollar-an-hour wage to retake the test.

I decided to meet him there to find out what was going on. Because of the language barrier, the Department of Motor Vehicles was sending him to an outsourcer to take his test. When I saw the neon sign out front, I knew something was off.

I asked for a manager and said, "This guy has taken his test three times and failed. What do we need to do to get him a license?"

The manager said that if William signed up for some special package, he would be guaranteed to pass. I swiped my card for $180, and magically William was approved for a license.

William's language barrier had left him helpless. It seemed that he'd actually passed his test, but for some reason they kept telling him he needed to come back. I wasn't sure that buying the special package was really necessary, but it was the quickest way to resolve the situation.

When I last ran into William, he was ecstatic. He's been able to share his story at the jail, and he got promoted at the museum because he could work a more flexible schedule. He is finally able to drive his family to church.

William needed a car, but what he really needed was an advocate.

It didn't cross my mind to ask, "Do you have a license?" If I need a license, I walk in, they snap a picture, and I answer eleven questions. Sadly, William was having 20 percent of his paycheck taken and was told he had to keep coming back.

Wow, the things I take for granted.

● ● ●

My experience with William was messy but was another example of how I can give to others. The money I paid for William to pass his driver's license test might not have been fair—they might have been taking advantage of him—but it was the easiest way to fulfill the gift for William.

I LIKE GIVING MY LIFE AWAY: JEREMY

Most people would think a retired elementary school principal like me would feel uneasy walking into the county jail.

I guess I've learned to feel comfortable in uncomfortable situations. Six years ago when the state arrested my friend's nineteen-year-old and put him in jail, his father and I began regular visits to the pod—an open, echoey corridor where on any given day you can find sixty-four inmates and a host of foul smells.

We began a Tuesday night study at the jail, and on Wednesdays I'd walk the rows and try to make friends. That's how I met a forty-eight-year-old inmate named Curtis.

I learned that Curtis's father died when Curtis was a child. To make ends meet, his mother bought a bar and raised her son in the company of vodka, beer, and loud music. Over the years Curtis developed an unshakable addiction to alcohol.

This wasn't his first time in jail. It was his thirty-fourth.

By the time I met him, everyone in Curtis's life had walked away—and rightly so. His wife, his children, even his state-appointed attorney had left him utterly alone, and both he and I knew it was entirely his fault. As I drew closer to him in friendship, though, I couldn't stand to let his past determine his future. There in the county jail, I decided to stick with Curtis.

In the months that followed, I attended hearings, met with judges, and searched for opportunities for Curtis outside the prison walls. I talked about my new friend with everyone in my life. I guess I couldn't help it. Though many people didn't understand why I'd spend so much time with a repeat offender, other people began to walk with him too. Without prompting, a local dentist offered to fix Curtis's teeth. Then an attorney offered to take his case.

In time Curtis was released from jail.

I remember driving him to a halfway house and watching him be turned away at the door. I remember inviting him to live with my family for two weeks until he found a place to stay. I remember watching him sweat with me in the fields as we dug holes for a new fence. As we worked, he joyfully waved at friends and family driving by in the sunshine. I remember smiling in his direction and feeling a sense of pride. By giving time to Curtis, I'd unknowingly given him access to the abundant relationships that had blessed my life too.

But there were also days when pride and compassion were replaced by total disappointment. Like the time I stopped by Curtis's new apartment only to find it littered with empty vodka bottles, bodily fluids, and trash. Or the days I got the calls informing me he'd been arrested a thirty-fifth time and then a thirty-sixth time.

Curtis hasn't stopped making mistakes, and it's possible he never will.

This may not be a success story when it's all said and done, but my idea of success may not be what this story is all about. After all, a relationship is about two people—not just one. In the last six years, I've come to realize that I'm not all that different from Curtis. How many times have I made the same mistake over and over again? How many times have I made decisions that could have landed me in his exact same place, behind bars? And through knowing Curtis, I've grown more patient, more compassionate, and more hopeful. After all, my compassion can't be directed by other people's decisions. Ultimately, it is not my responsibility to change Curtis. I can only love him the way I've been loved and treat him as I'd want to be treated.

People ask why I keep showing up when Curtis keeps

letting me down. But I just remember that Jesus does the same for me.

● ● ●

If you give, your gift might be wasted. Curtis accepted Jeremy's help and then turned around and betrayed his trust. If you choose to live a generous life, you choose to trust, and that trust might be broken at times. Your only other choice is to completely avoid giving to others, and if you do that, you're guaranteed to lose out on the joy generosity brings.

The choice is yours—choose to give or choose to play it safe. Jeremy kept choosing to give even after Curtis let him down. I've experienced some huge disappointments myself, but I keep choosing to give. There is no better way to live, and I know one thing for sure: without the risk of being let down, there is no chance of experiencing the rewards of the generous life.

I LIKE
NEW CAR SMELLS.

Submitted by: Steve

Confession: I like my stuff. Maybe that's why I was in my own little world of contentment as I clipped down the Chicago Skyway in my new Caspian blue metallic Volvo SUV.

The look is amazing, and the fit of those seats is perfect. And the smell. Nothing like drinking in that new car smell, and the smell of this Volvo is as luxurious as the rest of the vehicle.

I was heading downtown to an important meeting and was wearing one of my favorite suits, freshly cleaned and pressed. In my pocket was another favorite: my new iPhone. As I said, I like my stuff.

Contentment isn't something you think about too much when everything is going well, and I have to confess, it's been going quite well for my family and me. However, contentment becomes a conscious thought when some-body slams into it, which is exactly what happened as I was making my way toward downtown Chicago.

Everyone saw traffic slowing to a crawl. Everyone but Marie. I'd find out later that she was a working single mom, struggling to make ends meet, who lived at the edge of anxiety from the stress of it all. However, our introduction,

which came as a result of her clunker slamming into the rear end of my new Volvo, left me feeling less than sympathetic. Thank God nobody was injured, unless you count my bumper, which was totally trashed. Marie's clunker was just fine, except for the fact that it was still a clunker.

It was a surreal moment. We stood there looking at the damage as other commuters gawked at us as if we were a sideshow act.

We pulled our vehicles over to the shoulder. Trucks whizzed past, and I thought we needed to sort this thing out in a friendlier environment. I asked Marie and her young daughter to climb into my Volvo as we called for help. I certainly didn't see myself climbing into her car.

First I called the police. Then I asked if she was going to call her insurance company.

"I don't have any insurance," she said. "I had to let the coverage lapse. I couldn't afford the premium."

Of course you don't have insurance, I thought. I

maintained my composure but definitely could feel my temperature beginning to rise.

"Hey, maybe I could quickly call my insurance company to get them to restart the coverage," she said hopefully.

I didn't have the heart to tell her that probably wasn't going to work, but sure, whatever. "What's that? You don't have a phone and need to borrow mine?" *My brand-new, clean iPhone? Sure, why not. Could this get any more absurd?*

She connected with the customer service rep, and because the volume on both the phone and rep were set on high, I could hear both sides of the nearly thirty-minute conversation.

"It will cost three times the previous premium to restart the insurance because of the coverage lapse," the rep told her.

"I don't have that," Marie said. I could see tears beginning to fill her eyes. "I'll lose my license and won't be able to drive to work."

Great, I thought. *My new Volvo is trashed by a single mom who has no coverage on a clunker and whose kid is crawling all over my backseats. I'm now late for an important meeting, and the longer we sit here, the more I realize this lady smells.*

My patience had just about reached its limit when a thought hit me about as abruptly as her car had forty minutes earlier. It was as if God grabbed my shoulder and said, "Why don't you look at your life through the eyes of this lady and cut her some slack? The best thing you can do is let her out of this situation."

I suddenly realized I had thought of this as all about me and my new car, my new phone, my important meeting, and my convenience.

I felt properly chastised. I reached over, gently took the phone from Marie, and hung up the call.

"Why don't you get out of here," I said to her. "Why don't we just make this whole thing go away."

She was in shock. She gathered her small child, retreated to her car, and disappeared.

I disappeared too, planning to stop a few miles up the road and tie my bumper on so it wouldn't scatter pieces across the Skyway.

In that moment I realized I had been totally focused on me and my little program for a successful life. Thank God that he suddenly shifted my thinking to focus on Marie's desperate circumstances. What she needed was grace and forgiveness. I could afford to fix my bumper. She was on the verge of losing what little she had left.

As I drove down the toll road, I realized my new car smell had been replaced with something different, something better.

The fragrance of joy that comes from giving to others.

7
TACTICS

I believe that when giving is our idea, it makes us like giving. My hope is that you will give what you have decided in your heart to give, not reluctantly or under compulsion, but in freedom and joy.

Remember that giving is something you *get* to do, not something you've *got* to do. Giving promotes life and happiness. In fact, I've never met an angry and bitter generous person.

Simply start where you can, with what you have. There are so many needs in the world that if it were your job to meet them all, you would fail miserably every day and end up being miserable yourself. It's not your job to save the world. Don't fall for the trap of talking about how big and daunting the problems in the world are and doing nothing. You can't give what you don't have; you can give only what you do have, so start with that.

Leigh Anne and Sean Tuohy, whose family was the subject of the best-selling book and Hollywood movie *The Blind Side*, said, "We decided to take this approach: do small things with great love. If we could do that, little opportunities to give might grow beyond our wildest dreams."[8] By making yourself aware of opportunities to give, by following that nudge, you'll find satisfaction in knowing you are doing your part. Above all, don't let the enormity of the world's needs or any guilt trip rob you of the freedom to live a joyfully generous life.

As you continue on your journey, you might find yourself in situations that require a certain amount of creativity and interpersonal tact. If you aim to give to others in out-of-the-box and unexpected ways, you'll end up becoming a master of interpersonal communication and creative generosity. In this process you'll probably make some mistakes. I certainly have. That's fine. It's not like there's a giving police!

Don't be surprised if people are hesitant to receive a gift from you. When that happens, I just keep smiling and assure them I know I don't *have* to, but I *get* to.

People sometimes say, "You can't do that," to which I reply with a smile, "Oh yeah, I can."

Did I mention that sometimes I need to give more than other people need to receive? When I find myself getting caught up thinking about my life and my problems, giving sets me free from self-focus.

Sometimes I need to reassure the receiver that I want to give—a smile goes a long way in these situations. If people really want to reject my gift, I can't make them take it. From time to time that happens, and it's disappointing to be rejected, but ultimately you can't force a gift on someone.

If you're in a restaurant or a retail outlet and you don't want the person to know what you're up to, all you need to do is ask the appropriate person if he or she wants to get in on your giving conspiracy. Whether it's a manager, a waiter, or a clerk, get that person on your side by saying, "Hey, don't blow my cover on this one, okay?" People love that. They love to be in on something exciting.

Another way to surprise someone is to tip a person who doesn't normally get tipped. When you try this, be careful to send the right message. You want to honor the receiver. A smile goes a long way in sending the message: "You're worth this, and I want to give it to you." Our nonverbals help communicate a sense of worth. Give the gift of a tip *and* a smile.

Giving an unexpected tip is actually one of the most predictable ways to really throw someone for a loop. The expressions on people's faces can be priceless when you walk up to them with something for no other reason than to show them you appreciate their service.

I remember being with my daughter, Gracie, one day when we saw the mailman delivering our mail. I stopped the car and jumped out to give him a tip. He didn't know what to say. I told him I really appreciated his service and wanted to let him know. His expression said, "What's the catch?" So I had to reassure him there wasn't one. He came around and accepted my gift—I'm pretty sure it made his day. As we drove away, Gracie said, "I know what you did."

Surprising acts of generosity can get me into situations where the receiver is offended or just downright confused. Some people perceive that receiving a gift is an admission that they're weak and dependent. When you're giving, you need to be ready for that. Don't be surprised if they refuse at first. Be ready for the "you don't have to" line. Communicate the joy you get from giving, and set them at ease as you insist that it would make your day to give to them.

Another thing you need to be ready to do is give discreetly. Sometimes people have a personal need they feel ashamed about or don't want to call attention to. If you point out their need, you'll just make the situation worse, so think about a way to give that honors them and doesn't leave them feeling down.

Sometimes giving anonymously is the best tactic.

I LIKE WATER HEATERS: AMY

One day last winter I was talking with my friend Julie on the phone. She and I had met through our kids' second grade class and had become very close. I knew she was going through a difficult time and money was extremely tight. After four years serving in the air force, her husband was just finishing up his residency. In addition to the student loans and the daily costs of raising three young kids, Julie and her husband were dealing with the emotional and financial burdens of medical bills. One of their children was about to undergo major surgery. They were living on a shoestring budget, and she was overwhelmed.

"How can I pray for you?" I asked near the end of the conversation.

She paused a moment before answering, then said, "There is something our family needs prayers for right now. I know the hot-water heater needs to be replaced. We have no idea how we're going to pay for it. Our credit cards are maxed out, and I can't take any more loans from the bank or from family."

"I'll pray for you," I assured her.

Those words echoed in my head. *I'll pray for you.* Yes, I certainly would pray for Julie and her family, but I knew I could do something else for them as well. Hot water is a *must* during a Michigan winter. I immediately called my husband and told him about Julie's situation.

"They've been through so much, and I just want to love on them and bless them in any way we can," I said. "I think we should buy them a water heater."

My husband enthusiastically agreed. Early the next morning I called the heating-and-cooling company that had worked on our house. I explained that we wanted to give this water heater to Julie and her family but that I wanted to remain anonymous. The other end of the phone

line got really quiet. I thought the call had been discon-
nected and said, "Hello? Are you still there?"

"Yes, I'm here," the man answered. "I just—I just needed
a moment. Wow! What you and your husband are doing,
giving this family a water heater. That's not a call I get every
day!"

The day the water heater was installed, Julie called me
in tears. Her voice was filled with awestruck thankfulness,
and she was ecstatic as she talked about the surprise
water heater that had just been installed in her home. "You
won't believe what happened!" Julie exclaimed. "I know
you were praying, because your prayers were answered.
God is just taking care of us, and I am so blessed by this
gift and by this person, whoever it is. Someday when we
are able, we're going to bless someone back because
we are so grateful for this gift!"

It was a beautiful moment, rejoicing with my friend at
the blessings God had given and hearing her declare that
she would continue the generosity in her own way. Through
this whole experience I learned that blessings don't need
to be complicated. I only have to see where the needs are
and ask God how I can meet those needs.

● ● ●

What stands out to me about this experience is that,
while Amy's act of generosity certainly met a need of her
friend Julie, it impacted another life as well—the man at

the heating-and-cooling company. Don't you just love his response? Perhaps that day, due to his role in the giving experience, he was inclined to be generous himself. Perhaps her generosity sparked his thinking, and who knows what the ripple effect might turn out to be.

Another thing: Amy sensed that giving anonymously would best honor her friend, who was already deep in financial debt. Because the gift was anonymous, Julie was not burdened with a sense of shame or obligation. Giving is meant to enrich someone else, not to draw attention to that person's need.

When true generosity is your motivation, you'll find the best way to give while honoring the receiver.

Sometimes you get excited about giving to someone, but the timing isn't right. My approach is to follow the nudge and, when it comes, act on it. If there is doubt about the appropriateness of a gift, a few questions may help.

I LIKE IPHONES: BRAD

I had spoken with Joe over the phone a few times before I met him. I was in Oklahoma for a work related conference when we met for the first time. That was when I realized Joe was blind.

Joe and his wife invited me over for dinner. As we ate, Joe pulled out his cell phone—an older flip phone—and I was astonished that he could actually use the thing.

I'd heard that iPhones were especially useful for blind people because of different apps developed specifically for them. There are apps for counting money, detecting motion, identifying colors, and voice recognition. As I watched Joe mess with his flip phone, an idea started to take shape in my mind: maybe I could get an iPhone for Joe that would change his life.

As we ate, I asked him a few tactful questions. I slipped in a question about how happy he was with his service provider. He was very happy. How about his contract? It had already expired. *Okay*, I thought, *this might really work.*

On the drive back to my hotel, we took a detour to the AT&T store. Joe really didn't see it coming. We went inside, and Joe became overwhelmed with emotion as I told him I wanted to buy him a new iPhone. We took the time to pick out the right one together.

The salesman tried to sell Joe a phone with enough memory to store videos. Joe kindly pointed out that he wouldn't be watching any videos. The salesman gulped, "Oh, right," and wrote up the paperwork sheepishly.

The best moment was when we picked out the right cover for Joe's phone. Because he couldn't see them, I had to tell him what they looked like, and he had to trust me. As we stood in the store, I remember watching him run his fingers over the new cover—his way of "seeing" it.

It was a magical moment for me.

That was an experience I will never forget. Joe loves his phone; it's helped him immensely. I'm so glad I asked the right questions to discern whether the gift I wanted to give was right for him.

●●●

Learning to recognize that nudge to give and then asking a few questions has been a process for me. I still don't get it right every time, but a few tactful questions seem to help.

Of course, a gift doesn't need to be as large and expensive as a water heater or an iPhone. Just be mindful to be a blessing. Sometimes the perfect gift can look a little smaller—as small as a banana cream pie.

I LIKE BANANA CREAM PIE: SHANE

The day before Thanksgiving my wife sent me to a large grocery store with an even larger grocery list. Though she'd already texted me several times, reminding me not to forget the plastic utensils and to hurry home, I decided to make a slight detour. Last on the list was dessert. "Just some cupcakes or cookies," she'd said. "Nothing fancy." But I didn't want to bring home just any old dessert. I wanted a banana cream pie.

Next to the grocery store there was a small pie shop. Inside, glass cases housed rows of personal-sized chocolate, lemon meringue, blueberry, cherry, and peach pies. There were cheesecakes and key lime pies and every sweet filling that could ooze over a crumbling crust. When I finally spotted one banana cream pie, I rejoiced. It was the last one left, just for me.

I loaded up a dozen small pies and headed toward the checkout counter. But just then the bell on the front door jingled softly. A father and his three children walked in, talking merrily about what pies they might choose on this special trip. The man looked tired, but his youngest son walked directly past me and planted his hands on the case. With his nose touching the glass, eyes as wide as saucers, he exclaimed, "I know exactly what I want!" He looked up at the woman behind the counter. "Banana cream please!"

The woman answered gruffly, "We're out." And in that moment the boy's face morphed from pure glee to ultimate despair.

"You'll have to choose something else," his father explained.

Turning toward the boy's father, I admitted I was the culprit—I was the one who'd taken the last banana cream pie. I told him I'd be glad to give the pie to his son, but only on one condition: only if I could pay for their pies.

Immediately the man waved his arms in front of his body as if there was a bad smell in the air and said they couldn't possibly accept. He said he appreciated the gesture, but it wasn't necessary.

His son stood back, bewildered, arms at his side, eyes drooping in sadness. How could his father turn down a banana cream pie—and one that was free?

I explained once more that no strings were attached. That usually I like to give anonymously, but that today I wanted to give up my pie for his son. Reluctantly the father finally accepted.

When I handed the boy the last banana cream pie, he

held it in his hands delicately. He unsnapped the plastic top and sniffed the pie greedily. That smile he walked in with was back again. The pies purchased, the banana cream pie in the hands of its rightful owner, I strutted out the door.

That day I was as happy as that kid.

I LIKE
NURSING FEES.

Submitted by: Francis

Nursing school is hard, long, and expensive. After you spend several years in school, the journey ends with one comprehensive $200 exam: the National Council Licensure Examination. We call it NCLEX. Unless you've taken the NCLEX, you can't be a registered nurse, so during my time at Samford University's nursing school, teachers were constantly preparing us for that all-important test. It was exhausting!

I remember running my tired self into Walgreens for a quick errand one day during my sophomore year. I hoped

to grab a prescription and a few school supplies and then head across the parking lot to a coffee shop to study.

But that day things didn't go quite as planned.

As I checked out at the pharmacy counter, the cashier and I struck up a casual conversation. I explained that I was in nursing school, and the employee mentioned that her coworker—another young lady like me—had recently finished a nursing program too. I smiled cordially and pulled out my debit card to pay and be on my way.

But the cashier continued. "The problem is, she's been trying to keep up with her student loans and rent, and she can't seem to get enough money to pay for the licensure exam," the concerned employee said. "I actually just relieved her from her shift. She looked so exhausted."

I thought about the clerk's words and couldn't imagine working through all of nursing school, only to stop short of the final requirement: NCLEX. I expressed my sympathy for her friend's situation, and we finished our conversation and the transaction. I grabbed my bag, got back in my car, and drove to the coffee shop across the parking lot.

As I reached for my backpack full of books, notes, and a year's worth of knowledge, I stopped in my tracks. How could I get my stuff out to study, knowing that this young woman had worked so hard to persevere through nursing school but didn't have enough money to take the exam?

Without $200 to register for the NCLEX, she'd be stuck working at Walgreens, paying off student loans, and struggling to make her rent. Without that test she'd never have a chance to do what she'd worked so hard to do: care for other people in need. I knew I could afford to take a few extra moments out of my day and a few hundred dollars out of my bank account to meet a real and present need.

Turning my steering wheel as quickly as I could, I drove back to Walgreens. In the parking lot I wrote a check for $200, then walked back inside, scanned the greeting card aisle, and picked a card that said, "Congratulations!"

Back at the pharmacy counter, I asked my new friend for the name of her coworker, then wrote the name on the check. I slid the check into the card and sealed it, feeling a rush of excitement and adrenaline. When I handed the card to the cashier, she looked at me with amazement and said, "I can't believe it!"

A few weeks later I noticed that the check was cashed, and it made me smile. I'd never been happier to see $200 leave my bank account.

I LIKE SCARS.

Submitted by: Sarah

I was born with a condition called biliary atresia, and when I was three months old, my mother became a living donor, giving me 20 percent of her liver to save my life. I received the transplant and left the hospital with a large scar across my abdomen that looks something like the Mercedes symbol.

But this scar carried a lot more baggage.

You see, having a jagged mark that spans your entire waistline can be difficult to accept. While my friends were out buying bikinis and doing jumping jacks without fear in PE, I was covering up in a T-shirt and hoping to God that my scar didn't show. When it did, and someone shouted, "Ew! What's wrong with you?" the words cut deeper than the scalpel. I learned to hide my scar, fear the truth, and forget the past.

But everything changed when I was ten years old—the year I met Holly Walters.

Thanks to some encouragement from my parents, I'd decided to participate in the Transplant Games of America, a biannual event for athletes who have undergone

lifesaving transplant surgeries. When we arrived at the festival, I was amazed that the grounds were teeming with people just like me—people with scars, histories, surgeries, medications, and stories to tell. Sweat dripped from my brow as my parents and I joined a long line and waited under the hot Philadelphia sun to register for the track-and-field events. In front of me a tall, confident woman was complaining about the heat. Suddenly she lifted her shirt, hoping for some breezy relief. And that's when I saw the red, defacing triangular lines right across her belly.

The look of surprise on my face must have given me away, because the woman immediately introduced herself as Holly Walters. She learned that I too had survived a liver transplant. With excitement, she asked to see my matching scar. But I couldn't raise my shirt. I just couldn't let her see. I remember looking up at her and wishing I had her confidence, wishing I had that kind of courage.

Holly continued to pester me throughout the day, but I'd shake my head no. I watched her laugh and run and interact with so many people at the festival, and I felt this churning in my heart to be like her. How did she do it?

Then at the very end of the day, Holly finally convinced me, out of exhaustion, annoyance, or inspiration—I'm not sure which—to raise my shirt and show her my scar. When I did, she giggled and squealed and made me feel like I'd accomplished something huge. Looking back, I suppose I had.

"We're twins!" she exclaimed.

Her excitement was a gift. Her words told me there was no reason to be ashamed. Her scar showed me that I no longer needed to hide. Because the truth is, everyone has scars. Some are small and fading, others are deep and hidden within the tissue of the soul, and mine just happens to look like a Mercedes logo across my stomach. Thanks to Holly, I learned that I am beautiful just the way I am.

And now, every other year at the Transplant Games, Holly and I find each other to pose for one picture, baring two beautiful scars.

I LIKE
MY HIGH SCHOOL.

Submitted by: Leighton

I spent my whole life in a little town, learning from my parents—the most generous people I know—how to live.

As a child, I remember seeing the example they set and learning very early on that it is better to give than to receive. Once, when I heard about a family in need, I offered the only money I had to help: three measly dollars! But by the time I was graduating from high school, I'd set my sights on helping more than just one family. I wanted to help my entire high school learn about giving.

At any graduation, graduates do a lot of receiving. Gift cards, cash, well wishes, and a whole lot of advice about college. At my last graduation party, I was overwhelmed by the generosity of my friends and family, and I couldn't believe how much they blessed me with their giving. By the end of the summer, I'd come up with a plan for a portion of their gifts. I thought my plan could change the culture at the high school I was leaving behind. I had one last chance to make an impact.

I created an alias e-mail address and wrote an e-mail to the superintendent of schools with a simple idea. I would

leave $500 in twenty-dollar bills at the front office. Once a day until the money was gone, students could come by the office and take one twenty-dollar bill—no questions asked.

But there was a catch: they couldn't spend the money on themselves. The money was to be used to bless someone else—a friend who needed lunch, a homeless person they passed on the drive to school, a parent, or a neighbor. If they wanted, students could submit their stories of generosity to that same alias e-mail address. I knew that students might steal the money, but generosity is about trust, and I trusted that the students in my high school would live up to the challenge.

The day I left for college, I packed my car full of suitcases, clothes, and plastic furniture, excited about the adventure ahead. But before I hit the highway, I hit the ATM. I withdrew twenty-five twenty-dollar bills, wrapped them in an envelope, and drove to the high school. Just as the superintendent and I had agreed, I slipped the envelope under the office door and then walked away.

Over the next semester e-mails started rolling in with twenty-dollar stories, and every single one made my heart pump with excitement!

Some might think I'm crazy for giving my money to a group of high school students who will never know my name. But that wasn't the point. I didn't care about the money or my reputation or even where the dollars ended up. What I cared about was the legacy I left behind and the hope that even one high school student might give away twenty dollars, feel the rush of helping someone else, and start the habit of giving.

I LIKE GIVING MORE THAN I PLANNED.

Submitted by: Jim

A few years ago our church took on a service project, and I decided to get involved.

The plan was to renovate the house of a single mother. It was a gut-wrenching situation. Cindy's husband had walked out on her and their nine children. While she was in a panic, trying to figure out how to take care of all the children, her husband said to her, "You believe in God. Well, let God help you out."

Cindy and the kids were living in a dilapidated house, so a group from our church went over to see what exactly needed to be done. When we got inside, it was way worse than we'd thought. We would have needed to knock it down and start over. Several of her kids had health problems, probably from living in those conditions.

What she needed was a different house.

The course of the service project quickly took a dramatic shift. My wife and I talked it over and decided we wanted to buy a home for Cindy's family. I found a good deal on a nice house not too far from the one she was

living in and bought it. We did it through the church so she wouldn't know it was from us.

We spent four months updating the house and getting it furnished, and it turned out beautifully. When it came time for Cindy to move in, a group of us from the church came to help, so my wife and I got to be there.

I'll never forget what happened when they walked into their new home for the first time. One of Cindy's daughters looked up at her and asked, "Mommy, is this what heaven is going to be like?"

I'm an investor, so sometimes I lose a lot of money on a deal. Sometimes I find myself thinking, *Man, I wish I'd just given away that money to a better cause.* Years ago a friend challenged me with the idea of investing as much in ministry as I would in a good business deal. I hadn't considered that before, but when you think about it, which one has a better return? When someone wealthy tells me that he's bored or that she's lost her motivation to make money, I pass on this concept of looking at giving as a way of investing.

My wife and I have always given away a percentage of our money and had fun doing it. Then came the opportunity to do something bigger. We had simply gotten involved in a service project at the church, and the next thing we knew, we were looking in the face of a chance to buy a house for someone. We had to decide whether to step into it or walk away, because it was more than we had initially planned to do. When we stopped and thought about what really matters, it wasn't a tough choice. At the end of the day, giving is a way to actually invest in someone's life. We didn't want to miss out on the chance to do it for Cindy.

You certainly don't have to be a millionaire to make a difference. If you are, you may have greater opportunities than others, but the issue is not how much you have. It's what you do with whatever you have. That chance is in front of you. I urge you to take it. Giving someone a better life and a better future is one investment you will never regret.

THOSE WHO
REFRESH OTHERS
WILL THEMSELVES
BE REFRESHED

8
FAMILY

Embracing generosity as a lifestyle can become a healthy inspiration for those around you. For me, one of the most fulfilling aspects of giving has been watching generosity spread to my family. Earlier I wrote about how the work of I Like Giving started. Our family canceled our Sunday plans and went off on a wild adventure to give a family we had never met new bikes. The kids loved it so much they thought it was better than going to a water park for that day.

Today it is always fun for Laura and me when our kids surprise us with their ideas of generosity.

Recently Gracie came up to me and said, "Daddy, I have a problem." She grabbed my hand and walked me down the steps into our basement. "I have too many," she said as she pointed to the Mickeys and Minnies neatly arranged on her blanket.

Her perspective took me by surprise. And I thought of all the things I have. What are my stuffed toys? "Well, Gracie, you have a few options," I said. "You could keep them all. Or you could give some away." She walked into the playroom and pulled out her Minnie Mouse suitcase. She laid it on the floor, unzipped it, and carefully placed three stuffed Disney characters in the suitcase. After she finished zipping up her gift, she hurried over to me and gave me a great big hug. With tears running down her face, she said, "I feel so good. They are happy tears, Daddy."

Later that night after we had taken the gifts to the hospital, Gracie said, "Daddy, this is the best day of my life." Unforgettable.

But it wasn't always like that for our family. When I first started giving in unexpected ways, Laura really wasn't sure what to think. I'd watched my grandfather's example of lifestyle generosity, so it seemed natural to me. For Laura it was uncharted territory and a little scary. Since we share everything and make decisions together, she felt as if I was giving our money away without even asking. As you can imagine, that was a recipe for some interesting conversations.

Earlier I mentioned giving to an organization doing relief work in India. I loved writing them a check because it was my idea, and no one was telling me I should give to them. It was a breakthrough moment for me. But for Laura, it was a bit of a—how should I say this?—*surprise*. I'd sent the check from my office, so when the thank-you letter arrived at our house, Laura was caught off guard.

I had made a huge mistake. The truth is, I had started giving to other organizations and people as well—all without her knowing about the gifts. Can you imagine the look on her face when someone came up to her and thanked her for a gift she had no idea she had given?

I realized that if we were going to give, we needed to do it together. We decided we would set limits on how much we could give without talking to each other first.

This changed things. Now that we were on the same page, there was a new unity and shared excitement in giving. We took time to explore giving opportunities together, even traveling to other cities to learn more about organizations that caught our interest. Getting to meet the people behind the scenes and understanding their work helped us in our decision-making process. This also brought a new richness to our lives and our marriage.

As we gave, we discovered more of the mysteries of each other's heart. I loved being able to support the work in India, while Laura found life in giving to ministries that helped girls with addictions, eating disorders, and unplanned pregnancies. I was unaware of that type of ministry, but realizing it was meaningful to her, we gave in that way too.

Soon our life of giving together was going to move to an entirely new level.

We had bought a convertible; we thought it was the perfect car. One day as I was jogging around our neighborhood, I kept passing the convertible and thinking, *Everything about that car is right.* I must have taken one pass too many, though, because all of a sudden I was hit by a powerful impression.

That nudge. I knew I was supposed to give the car away.

Hoping it was just a random thought, I mentioned it to Laura, and I was thankful she didn't feel the same way. We'd learned to be in agreement about decisions like these, so I categorized it as a scary feeling and nothing more.

But I was unable to let it go.

A few weeks later Laura confirmed what I had felt. Our oldest son, Danny, who was five at the time, chimed in on the car conversation. He asked his mom what she thought about giving the car away. After considering it for a while, Laura decided she thought it was right. There was a sense then that we were entering into something bigger than ourselves. Even though we loved that car, we were excited to see what adventure giving it away might bring.

I took the car to the local dealer and explained that we wanted to sell it and donate the money to the group we supported in India. The dealer seemed intrigued and agreed that, as long as I paid the commission, he would be happy to sell it for me. After running some inspections, he told me it would cost an extra $1,500 in repairs before it would be ready to sell. I gulped. *Seriously? I'm selling this car to send the money to other people, and now I have to pay to make it perfect for the next owner?* I was committed, so I paid for the repairs, and the car was put on the lot.

Months went by, and nothing happened. Winter came and went, and not a single buyer showed any interest in the car. Had we made a mistake? Was this all really just a crazy idea? The doubts crept in, but we stayed strong and hoped a buyer would arrive.

Finally, late in the spring, one of the managers at the dealership called me and recommended that we take it to a local car auction. I thought about it for a minute and decided that selling the car really wasn't primarily about the money but about our hearts, so I agreed. Even if the car sold for less than it was worth, it was the right thing for us to do. We all loved that car, but our hearts were being prepared to put the needs of others first. Even so, I felt it would be a waste if it sold for too little.

The auction started. The bidding priced our beloved convertible well below wholesale.

Then all of a sudden something amazing happened.

Honestly, it was one of those pinch-yourself moments; it seemed surreal. Two people started bidding as if our car were the hottest item in town. I mean, where did that come from? The bidding shot up quickly to a few thousand dollars *over* retail. We watched in disbelief as a dealer paid more than he could sell it for.

Later we found out that he had promised his wife he would get her a convertible and was willing to pay almost any price!

How awesome is that? We were amazed at how the car sold, and it was a privilege to be able to send the money to India. But more important than the money was the lesson it taught us about letting go. Even though we enjoyed that car, we've never regretted giving it away and the adventure it brought.

Giving will certainly remove boring from your life!

Including our kids in giving adventures like that shows them a better idea of what generosity can look like. We don't want to make them feel obligated, so we have found ourselves looking for ways to model generosity and to invite them into it.

On the local level this has included spending time and volunteering as a family at various organizations in our city, serving meals, packing lunches, sorting clothes, or just spending time with others. We have also found ways to be involved with local needs in our neighborhood and in our schools.

On the international level, when our kids turned six, each one picked out a child to sponsor through Compassion International. The sponsorship is ongoing and includes praying, writing letters, and sending small gifts in the mail. We also look forward to contributing to their college education as they grow up. It's been a great way to make a real connection between our family and children in need. We were able to meet and visit the home of one of our children in Ecuador. That up-close and personal experience will forever be etched in our children's minds.

We also have set up a "giving jar" in the house for any time our kids want to contribute some spare change. As the jar starts to fill up, the conversation turns toward how we can share it. One day our children set up a lemonade stand in our neighborhood. With the stand open for business, they taped pictures of their Compassion children on the front of the card table for their customers to see. Not only did they raise money to send to their Compassion children, but they raised awareness in our neighborhood of the organization. Several families went on to sponsor their own children! When our kids embrace generosity without any prompting, Laura and I know that our modeling is paying off.

I like to say that in our family we have the giving conversation on the seven-year-old level, the eleven-year-old level, and the fifteen-year-old level. As our kids grow, we bring them in on more details of our giving decisions.

One thing I've learned through the process is that I can't force generosity. I can't lead my family unless I'm going there myself. Simply keeping my eyes open for opportunities to give and ways to include the whole family sparks the idea in my kids. Kids are too young and innocent to believe they can't be generous if they see adults living that way.

When we started making videos for I Like Giving, our

first video was a story called "I Like Bugshells." It was about Bella, the daughter of my friend Mark, deciding to spend her Saturday collecting pop cans so she could send money to World Vision. Together with a friend and her mom, Bella raised $67.60 to help people who don't have access to clean drinking water. The best part was that it was entirely her idea.

I believe giving is built into all of us. We are wired to give. But if the desire to give isn't nurtured when we are young, it can dry up and die. Once people start giving, it tends to stick. Laura and I feel as if we are significantly affecting our family's legacy and inheritance through generosity. It is as if we are doing something very real to our future family tree.

The other day as we were talking with our kids, they were recalling several giving stories that Laura and I had completely forgotten. We looked at each other and realized that their minds are like steel traps for these stories.

This is a sobering responsibility. I never want to underestimate the example I am setting. My kids are watching how I live, and the choices I make have rippling effects down through the generations. I can choose to do nothing and let my children be swept up in the current of empty materialism that is rampant in our culture, or I can choose to live a different way by living generously.

This is not just theory. It's working. I see the effects of our life choices showing up regularly in my kids' lives.

Giving is learned. About a year ago Gracie surprised us with what has become one of my favorite giving stories yet.

I LIKE SPARKLY NAIL POLISH: LAURA

For my six-year-old daughter, Gracie, sparkly anything was a big deal. For weeks she'd been saving sparkly stickers on her sparkly behavior chart to have enough to earn sparkly nail polish as a reward. When she had saved enough, we took a trip to one of our favorite stores, Target, to pick out the perfect polish.

We arrived at the store and headed to the cosmetics department, where Gracie took her time considering her options. As we stood there, we noticed a couple of older girls nearby. They were eying a more expensive bottle of designer nail polish and seemed to be pooling their resources to buy it. Money was literally falling on the floor as they pulled it out of their pockets, but as we overheard them talking, we realized they didn't have enough.

Holding a bottle of nail polish in her hands, Gracie looked up at me and smiled. I assumed she was happy because, unlike the older girls nearby, she *did* have enough to buy her nail polish.

Then something totally unexpected happened.

Gracie motioned for me to lean down close to her face. She whispered in my ear, "Mommy, I think we should buy the nail polish for them."

I'll admit I was a little taken aback. As a family, we've always tried to be aware of the needs of others and help where we can, but it had been more of a challenge with Gracie than with our other kids. Being six years old, our only girl, and frankly a little spoiled, Gracie was not one I expected to demonstrate the spirit of generosity so soon.

Of course, I thought it was a great idea. I rolled up a ten-dollar bill and handed it to one of the girls, telling her we wanted them to be able to buy the nail polish they wanted. They were surprised and initially weren't sure they could accept it. But we insisted that we wanted them to take the money and enjoy the nail polish they had their eyes on.

Gracie, who had been watching while I delivered the spontaneous donation, took my hand and led me to another, more private aisle. "Mom," she said, absolutely beaming, "that was so fun!"

I was so proud of her and told her so, but she had something more in mind.

"Mom," she said, "we have to do high/low tonight!"

Often over dinner our family shares the highlights and lowlights of our day. Gracie was so excited about the sparkly nail polish gift that she couldn't wait to tell the family about it.

As we continued to shop, she skipped around the store behind me with joy. It wasn't until we were back in the car that it hit me—we had forgotten to get *her* nail polish, and she hadn't even mentioned it!

To this day, months later, Gracie still hasn't said a word about the nail polish she didn't get. Rather, she likes to mention, as we pass the nail polish section in Target, the memory of our sparkly nail polish gift.

As a mom I try to encourage my kids to be helpful and generous, but there is something so magical when it comes from them in unexpected ways. Since that day I've realized I need to be more open to spontaneous acts of generosity from my children and willing to go along with them when they happen.

A gift of nail polish might be a little thing, but the reward of seeing a giving opportunity and seizing it, no matter how small, is such a joy!

●●●

Yes, my heart does swell with pride when I hear that story. It was just one of those moments that took Laura and me by total surprise, and it was so fun to see how Gracie *loved* the experience.

Sometimes giving can be a joint effort too. It's awesome when our kids come up with ways to give without prompting from us, but that doesn't mean we never give them an idea. In the next story you'll see what I'm talking about. My son Danny had started a business in the neighborhood and was earning a pretty good income for his age. One morning, without any intention of being prescriptive, I showed him something in the newspaper. It moved his heart so much he decided to put his earnings toward helping someone else. When he told me his plan, I agreed to match him dollar for dollar so we could be in it together and I could boost his efforts.

It was a fantastic experience.

I LIKE SMILES: DANNY

A few years ago I started my own business. I began the old-fashioned way, going door to door, introducing myself, and offering my services. I kept knocking until I lined up twelve accounts. I was ready to work hard and watch the profits roll in.

I was eight.

My clients were thrilled. It was wintertime, and for one dollar I would shovel the snow off their sidewalks until the pavement showed through. I imagined what I would do with my earnings. All those dollar bills would stack up tall. The sky was the limit. I waited with anticipation for the first snow to fall.

Before it did, before my work even began, my dad and I were sitting at the table eating breakfast. He slid the morning paper across the table and said, "Whaddaya think about this?"

Right in the middle of the sports highlights was a black-and-white advertisement. It was for Smile Train, the international charity that helps kids in desperate need of a simple cleft-palate surgery.

Once I saw the ad, I could not unsee it. I looked at a particular picture—one of a girl named Amalia. It was as if she were looking back at me. She seemed so helpless. I thought, *What if that was me?*

Immediately I knew what I was going to do. I was going to help the helpless. I was going to save Amalia.

The surgery cost $250. My dad said he would match me dollar for dollar, so it was up to me to make $125.

That winter it snowed. A lot. I didn't realize how hard the shoveling would be. It was so cold. Instead of sitting in my cozy house, I was standing in snow up to my kneecaps trying to dig my way to the bottom. As soon as I got one sidewalk done, it would snow again. I didn't want to do it anymore. I wanted to be inside drinking hot chocolate. I thought about my dad and how maybe he could pay for the whole thing himself. But I knew he would tell me to keep going, and I knew he would be right.

Well, 125 sidewalks later, I had finally done it. It took the entire winter season. It took all my profits. It took everything.

When I got out that white envelope and smoothed the stamp over it, I felt so full. I knew there was one little girl who would have a smile on her face.

It's easier to live life trying not to see things. To think it's all about you. But it's not. There's a whole world out there. You just have to open your eyes and see it. There are opportunities all the time, but you only get one life. Why not spend it making a difference in somebody else's?

I close my eyes and picture Amalia smiling.

I am smiling too.

●●●

Danny could have worked hard all winter and saved for new clothes or a trendy gadget. The problem with buying things is that they fade with time. Giving a gift, on the other hand, sticks with us forever. Danny chose to do something life changing with his money. Because he did, he has a story that will last.

We are learning as a family that giving involves more than things or money. It can be a listening ear, a touch, or simply the gift of time.

I LIKE THE FLAG: DREW

I'm just a kid. But I don't think I have to wait until I'm big to do big things. My dad has a lot of ideas about ways we as a family can make a difference. Some of them sound a little crazy. Like today when he said, "Let's go to the veterans' home."

I wasn't even sure what that was. I wasn't sure about going to a place I had never been before. I wasn't sure what I would say or how I would feel. There was actually a lot I wasn't sure about. But we went anyway.

We showed up and entered a room about the size of our kitchen. Our kitchen is new and clean and has great food. This kitchen was old and stale and had food I would never eat. There were a few people quietly sitting about, one who caught my eye.

His name was Fred. He was probably in his sixties. He

was seated in a wheelchair wearing some tattered jeans and a US Navy hat, cigarette in hand, ready for a light. I wondered what adventures those legs had taken him to before they met that chair.

He was heading out for his smoke, so we asked if we could go with him. We followed him to a spot where he had been many times before. It was out back and overlooked a creek surrounded by dozens of acres and trees. Strung between two tall oaks was an American flag proudly swaying in the breeze. With an outstretched arm he pointed to it and in his gruff military sort of voice said, "Do you know what that flag means?"

"Freedom," I said.

"You're darn right," he said as he took a big puff of his smoke. He went on to tell us all sorts of stories about the war, about the characters he'd met and the bullet he'd survived—the one that ricocheted off the tree and hit him in the neck. He even taught me how to salute the flag with his hand so firm and stiff it seemed it could slice right through that cigarette.

I thought about Fred and all the others who had sacrificed so much for that flag, for freedom, for us. I thought about this veterans' home and the wheelchair and what they were receiving in return. This random group of people united by red, white, and blue were so special, but it seemed they were being forgotten. I wondered if I was the only one to visit Fred. I wondered if this was the best we could do.

I showed up today feeling as if I didn't have much to offer. It turns out that I was able to offer the only thing that was really needed.

Fred was a book of stories waiting for an audience. Sometimes people don't need money or skills or advice. They just need someone to hear their stories and witness their lives. The simple words *hello* and *thank you* went a lot further than I realized.

As we were leaving, we had almost reached our car as we heard Fred yell out, "You made my day!"

I was actually thinking the same thing. Cigarettes, bullets, and stars—all this in one day!

I LIKE
POTTY TRAINING.

Submitted by: Missy

If I said there was a link between world hunger and potty training, do you think you'd get the connection?

No, I wouldn't have either, but anyone who has kids knows you never know what's going through the mind of a child.

Maybe I should explain.

My son has an appetite like a football player's, or at least he thinks he does.

He's three.

He talks about how hungry he is—he's always eating—but too often he'll take only two or three bites of something, and then he's done with it. We've been trying to get him to understand that he can't do that, that it's wasteful. We've been talking a lot about how children his age in other parts of the world barely have enough food to survive and that many don't have any food at all.

"Mommy," my three-year-old said one day, "we need to help them."

And that's where the link between world hunger and potty training comes in. We were in the throes of making the transition out of diapers and had been having varying degrees of success. He was wearing Pull-Ups but would get lazy and just go potty in them if he didn't want to get to the bathroom.

So when he said we needed to help hungry children, I said, "Well, we could use the money Mommy and Daddy are using for diapers if you start going potty in the potty."

It worked!

It isn't the most sophisticated way to help kids in Africa, but he was suddenly and enthusiastically motivated to become potty trained. Now we sponsor a four-year-old boy in Uganda. We have his picture on the refrigerator, and our son shows everyone who comes to our house his picture and tells the little boy's story.

I never would have thought there'd be a connection between world hunger and potty training, but we couldn't be more excited that our son saw it as a way to give to someone who needed help.

9
COMMUNITY

One of the things I love most about generosity is that it ripples. It spreads out into the world—into our families, our communities, and our work—and has immeasurable effects.

A while back Drew had a group of friends over, and we were all playing in the yard together. We were playing catch, and I decided I'd spice it up a bit by offering twenty-five cents for each catch. Then, just for fun, I added a little more to the fire by saying that if the ball was tipped and then caught, I'd fork out fifty cents. Of course the boys loved it, and there was a rush of energy and competition. We had a great time, and everyone competed fiercely for those tipped fifty-cent catches. At the end of the game, we were all exhausted, and I had a good amount of quarters to pay out.

I stood there in amazement as, without any prompting

from me, Drew walked past the giving jar on his way to the garage and put his winnings into it.

As his friends followed him, each one did the same thing!

I was struck by that experience, not only because of the generosity of my son and his friends, but because I could imagine each of his friends going home and telling his parents about it. Those conversations could start ripple effects in each boy's family.

I don't think we can ever overestimate just how profound the effects of giving can be. You can give without loving, but you can't love without giving. The reality is that other people are watching how we live our lives, and what we do can have extraordinary effects in our communities.

Generosity is for all of us. It is available to all of us, even when the cultural tide is moving in the opposite direction. Why not be brave and live differently?

As you grow in generosity, your ability to spot opportunities will grow. After talking to people about giving for a while, I realized that a lot of my friends wanted to experience the joy I had found but weren't sure where to start. So when an opportunity popped up, I decided I'd put it out there and see who was interested.

Sandy drove the bus that took our kids to school, and we'd enjoyed getting to know her. She had been battling cancer and other health issues, and we realized she could really use some time to rest and recover. Laura and I talked about it and decided we wanted to pay for Sandy to take a trip to Florida so she could be away and relax. I realized this could be a perfect opportunity to get some friends in on the giving, so I called a few whose kids were on Sandy's bus route and told them what I was thinking.

Some tact was involved in making the offer. I didn't want it to feel like an obligation, so I just lobbed it out there. I said something like "Hey, we're looking at doing this, and we're thinking of doing it ourselves, but we just wanted to see if anyone else wanted in." It wasn't a request, just an invitation that could be easily declined. I didn't even ask for a specific amount. Before I could finish casting the whole vision, they were all in.

One of my friends who does a lot of planned, programmatic giving told me he had been wanting to give in this way but didn't know where to start. He was so excited he said, "Wow, I almost missed this. Thank you so much for thinking of me!"

I guess you can call that "*We* Like Giving!" Sandy likes to call it "I Like Florida."

I LIKE FLORIDA: SANDY

I walked into the hospital on Valentine's Day thinking I had appendicitis. I was thirty-one, married, and had two young children. Later that day I was diagnosed with uterine sarcoma and walked out of the hospital a cancer patient.

I learned to cope with the side effects of my chemotherapy and radiation. For years things went on normally. I was a preschool teacher, and every day I drove the school bus to and from the homes where my students lived. I did my best to ignore the growing tingling in my right leg and continued with my work as best I could.

Years after my original brush with cancer, I was driving my bus when I felt my right leg—my driving leg—go numb. I radioed the other driver, and we drove back to school one behind the other. From there I rushed to the emergency room.

I remember when the technician came back into the room holding my x-rays; his face was ghost white. I'd seen that look before. They'd found another cancerous mass— this time in my right leg.

The next few months were grim. My father was diagnosed with pancreatic cancer, and as I watched my dad suffer and ultimately lose *his* battle with cancer, I couldn't help wondering what was going to happen in *my* life. I didn't want to die.

I underwent a risky surgery at the Mayo Clinic. Doctors informed me of all the possibilities: I might lose my leg, I might not walk again, I might not even wake up from surgery. But in a miraculous turn of events, I left the hospital with my leg and my life. I started on the road to recovery.

I remember mentioning to my daughter in the midst of a harsh winter that it would be so nice if I could recover in a warm place.

A few weeks later my daughter went to tutor at a family's house. As it turned out, one of their children was in my preschool class and had been on that school bus the day of my emergency. While my daughter was at their home, the dad asked her a simple question: "Do you think your mom would like to stay in a place in Florida for a little while?"

Of course when he called and offered to pay for the trip in full, I was overwhelmed. It's not that my husband and I couldn't afford a trip to Florida. We could have. It wasn't the money that surprised me. It was the flights, the car rental, the hotel, all the details and decisions—I never would have had the energy or strength to plan a vacation even though it was the exact retreat I needed. He told us all we had to do was pack and get on a plane.

After all I'd been through, I never imagined someone might give us a gift that was so restorative. When we arrived in Florida, I couldn't help but meet every person sitting around the pool beside me. I'd share with them the story of the school bus, and I'd share with them the story of abundant generosity.

Looking back, I can see that my trip to Florida was more than a vacation. It changed my view on giving. Now I'm always looking for ways to be on the other end of an extravagant gift.

●●●

Inviting friends to come together and bless someone in our community was an amazing experience. By giving to

Sandy we were able to be generous to someone in our community *with* people in our community.

A simple story can be refreshing and empowering. Stories connect people, and they give people permission to try new things. I call it the power of story. Telling giving stories can center people on what matters most and bring them back to a healthy balance in life. The cultural current often pulls us in the direction of self-focused living and empty materialism. If we do nothing, we just drift along with it. Giving stories can help us avoid that drift and move us toward doing things for others instead.

Just the other day I was meeting with the I Like Giving team when I got a text from a friend who works in downtown Grand Rapids. He thanked me for the latest I Like Giving film and said that every time he sees one of our stories, it centers him on what matters most.

Of course, not everyone gets excited about giving stories. Some people think I'm trying to guilt-trip them or tell them how to live their lives. Others may fear that generosity could shake up their usual, comfortable routines. Hopefully, by now you know that I don't tell other people where to give their money.

Sadly, there can also be hurtful aspects to living generously in your community. People may try to take advantage of your good will.

I remember taking a friend to a clothing store a few years ago. He was serving with a nonprofit, and I wanted to support his work by giving him some new clothes. We went into the store, and I gave him a budget for how much I would like to spend. It was all going well and was a lot of fun when, after we had reached our limit and were paying, he piled on a few more items of clothing and said, "I think we could get these too."

Instantly the whole experience moved from joy to manipulation. I felt taken advantage of. It hurt. After another similar experience with the same man, I found myself pulling away from the friendship. It was disappointing, but, as I said before, giving can open you up to being disappointed. That relationship soured, but I didn't stop living generously—that would have robbed me of my own joy.

I see the possibilities of generosity strengthening relationships and building community. It opens people's eyes to others around them. It prompts the question "Can I do something for them?" It also allows people to show their weakness and know that others around them will help if they can.

It can be a beautiful thing.

One day I was speaking at a church, and I noticed a man intently looking at me with his arms crossed tightly against his chest. As I began to share stories of people finding joy through acts of generosity, Mr. Arms-Crossed-Guy's demeanor changed. Pretty soon his arms were unfolded and his head wasn't leaning back. By the time my talk was over, he was leaning forward with his ears tuned in! The following week I received a story called "I Like Holiday Inn Express."

I LIKE HOLIDAY INN EXPRESS: BILL

I am a road warrior.

No, not like the one found in Mel Gibson's 1979 post-apocalyptic movie that features guys with severe road rage doing battle with muscle cars. I'm more like a sales representative who travels a lot of miles and stays in hotels.

I was exhausted on the Monday night I checked into a Holiday Inn Express. As I headed to the reception desk, I passed a woman on her phone. I noticed her kids, three boys between the ages of about ten and fifteen, all sitting quietly, reading books. I could tell by her phone conversation that she was talking to a friend and trying to get together some money for a night in the hotel. I asked the desk clerk what the story was. She said the lady was on her way to Chicago, and she and her kids were fleeing from an abusive situation at home. Apparently it was a "grab the keys and get out of there" circumstance.

Normally, I wouldn't have been so inquisitive, but I had just heard a presentation the day before in my church about being generous to other people and becoming more aware of opportunities to do something kind for someone else. I quietly told the receptionist I'd pay for their room. I also realized that they probably didn't have money for food or gas. I gave the clerk $250 to give to the family so they could eat.

The next morning, I received this note:

> Dear Sir,
>   I don't even know what to say. I know you want

to remain anonymous, but I need to tell you how much I appreciate what you did for my family. That morning I prayed, "God, if you are real, now would be a good time to show up." I can't believe it.

Thank you so much!

I've done similar things since helping that family, and I've found there are opportunities everywhere! The key for me has been to stop focusing on myself and pay attention to what is going on around me. You can't help everybody, but you can help somebody.

● ● ●

Bill's heart was softened through the power of story combined with a courageous decision to listen and respond to a need. The effects of this in his own life go even further than this story and the others he alluded to. It changed him. Bill's pastor later told me that after the Holiday Inn experience, Bill came to him and apologized. He said he had stopped giving to the church a few years ago because he was miffed about a capital campaign that didn't go as he thought it should. He realized that he had robbed himself of the joy of giving all this time, and now he was ready to give to the church again—with joy.

Duty, guilt, and obligation did not move him to act. Being softened by the power of story and then courageously listening and responding was what prompted the shift and brought him freedom to experience the joy of giving! This heart change is exactly why *I Like Giving* works with pastors to inspire a culture of generosity in churches across the country.

In a similar way, generosity in the business community brings significant benefits to the employees and owners. I love the culture at Trek bikes. They came up with a creative idea to give an employee a gift he will never forget. It all started with hard work and a leader who remembered a little detail in his employee's life.

I LIKE GUITAR: STEVE

I have a young employee who works really hard. He is a great guy who always gives 110 percent, and we all really appreciate him. Outside of work he is a passionate guitar player, and for months he had been talking about a new Martin guitar that he was saving for. I recently asked him how much more he needed to save to get this "dream guitar" he kept talking about. His response? Fifteen hundred dollars. Wow, this must be some guitar!

I couldn't get it out of my mind, so I met with his direct supervisor, who reports to me. We decided to put this awesome employee in for a bonus in the amount of, you guessed it, $1,500. Upon receipt, he was blown away to the point of near tears. It was an amazing experience to look for creative ways outside our traditional bonus system to give to one of our hardworking employees.

I was reminded of the power of listening. I want to listen

to my employees' hopes and dreams, and perhaps there will be more opportunities to be generous with them. This young employee felt heard and known. He is now working harder than ever for our company, and we had a blast doing something a little unusual that absolutely worked!

●●●

I love this story because I can imagine the lasting impact one gift had on Steve's employee and the impact it will have on Steve's business for years to come.

We all know that the culture we create in our businesses, whether as an employee or a leader, is so important to success. But have you considered what a culture of generosity might do for your business? At I Like Giving we work with businesses to transform culture, because we know that a culture of generosity means more engaged employees, higher levels of productivity, and more satisfied clients.

It's really hard to find a community that generosity can't make better.

Take a minute to think about your life. Do you feel secure and loved in a community of people you can trust? Are your weaknesses complemented by other people's strengths? Do you feel able to give in the unique ways that are your strengths? Could small acts of generosity enrich your life relationally? How could you incorporate generosity into your interactions with the people you see during the day?

I LIKE
TRUMPETS.

Submitted by: Dale

I'm a police officer in Jacksonville, Florida, so I interact with a lot of people around the city and see many different types of needs.

One time a fellow officer told me the heart-wrenching story of an underprivileged child in junior high whose trumpet had been stolen. This was a kid who loved music and lit up when he played. He was extremely disappointed that he did not have a trumpet, but he so wanted to continue learning to play that he refused to quit band class.

The school did not have a trumpet to loan him, and his family couldn't afford to replace the stolen trumpet. Week after week he kept coming to class. As the rest of the band played around him, he carefully practiced the notes on an imaginary trumpet.

When I heard about the boy's commitment, I was compelled to do something. I reached out to other officers in the area and gathered donations. We collected enough to purchase a new trumpet for this child. I found one online, ordered it, and couldn't wait for the package to arrive. I took it to my fellow officer, who in turn gave it to the child.

I later asked Officer Wyatt about the boy's reaction. He said the boy kept looking at the trumpet and looking back up at Officer Wyatt in disbelief. It's not every day that you see tears of joy in the eyes of a teenage boy.

That was several years ago. I still wonder if I will ever hear him play. But whether or not I do, it's fun to think about him playing real notes on a real trumpet somewhere.

Many times in my life I've heard about a need that I didn't have the money to meet. Yet I have realized I can still play a part in giving. All I did was tell others about a need, and they responded. Some of them even came back later and thanked me for the opportunity to be part of something meaningful.

As police officers, we are here to help the public. It's what we do. A lot of things happen behind the scenes and go unnoticed, but that's fine with us, because we're not looking for a pat on the back. We do what we can because it's the right thing to do. And if what we do affects someone's life for good, that's all we need to know.

I've read stories about people doing things for others that have sparked a desire in me to live more generously. I'm sharing this story in the hope that it causes someone else out there to take action.

If you don't have the money to meet a need yourself, don't let it stop you. You can still participate in giving, simply by facilitating it.

10
RECEIVING

Something happens inside me when I give. An incredible feeling wells up within my soul and makes me feel more alive. When I choose to give with no strings attached and no sense of obligation, I have the sense that I am valuable, that I am needed, and that I make the world a better place.

When someone gives to me, I have a different feeling. Receiving can be harder than giving, because receiving reminds me that I need other people. When someone meets a legitimate need that I am unable to meet on my own, I'm humbled. When someone gives me a gift for no reason other than wanting to give to me, that can be deeply moving. Receiving is very different from giving, but if you're going to become a good giver, it will serve you well to become a good receiver too.

We're often told that the best way to live is to be

independent and strong. We're told to pull ourselves up by our bootstraps (however that works), work hard, and never admit that we need anything. Being weak can be seen as shameful, and receiving from others can make us feel we've failed at life.

But is weakness really that bad? Could it be that our specific weaknesses allow other people's strengths to shine? Could it be that life sometimes throws us a curve that creates a need in our own lives for others to help?

Once you experience the joy of giving, you realize that other people feel the same way when they give to you. Receiving might be harder than giving, but if you think about the joy the givers are receiving when they give to you, that will help you open up to receiving. You know that refusing the gift would deny them that joy.

I think one of the things about giving to others when there is no obligation is that it reminds them they are worthy of love. They didn't have to earn it; they are inherently worthy.

Another frequent result of receiving is the desire to turn around and give to others. Giving is contagious. Think back to the story of Tracy Autler at the beginning of this book. Imagine if she had refused that Thanksgiving dinner. What would have happened if she had turned up her nose and said no to her neighbor's kindness? I doubt she would have become the generous person she is today. But she didn't refuse. She said yes, and that started a sequence of events that drew her into a generous lifestyle. As a result, thousands of others have received from her since then.

Receiving well also honors the giver. Margot, the lady who gave to Tracy, was debilitated by her multiple sclerosis, but imagine the joy and worth she felt, knowing she had made Tracy's Thanksgiving Day.

A friend spoke to me recently about receiving. He said that receiving broke down some of the resistance that had built up in his heart over the years. He is an immigrant, and living in a foreign country has often been difficult. At times he's felt marginalized because he is culturally different. Lately he has been the recipient of great generosity, and it's had a profound effect on his life. He now feels valued in situations where he felt neglected before.

But he could have chosen to refuse. He could have chosen to say no to receiving and let his heart stay hard. Because he didn't, he is experiencing greater richness in his own life and is becoming more generous himself.

Generosity can do that if we are willing to open ourselves to receiving from others.

I heard it said that a person with a good heart cares for widows and orphans. This gave our family the desire to look for those types of giving opportunities. We realized we didn't know anyone who was widowed, so I asked my hairdresser if she knew any. She said she did and acted as my go-between. Our family started sending anonymous checks to her friend who was a widow.

Years later I had the privilege of meeting Evelyn. As it turned out, our generosity to her had translated into her generosity to others. (Also, the lady who cut my hair was so moved by what I was doing that I haven't paid for a haircut since!)

I LIKE HAIRCUTS: EVELYN

When you're ninety-seven years old like me, life moves slowly. But it keeps moving. That's been my philosophy for quite some time, and it's why thirty years ago, when my husband and I retired, I didn't stay at home to live my last days in quiet comfort. Instead, I volunteered at a food pantry and the veterans' hospital, helped my neighbors run errands to the grocery store, and did whatever I could to be useful. I guess it's my nature. I can't sit down and let others do the work when I know I'm fully capable.

I kept that mind-set even as life grew more difficult. My husband passed away twelve years ago, and even though we'd saved for retirement, by the time he was gone, so were our savings. For a few years I made ends meet through Social Security and tried not to let the dwindling number in our bank account stop me from regularly visiting the veterans' hospital. During that time the only extravagance I allowed myself was a regular trip to see Carol at the salon. I'd known Carol for forty years, and when she cut and styled my hair, she made me feel beautiful. Somehow that helped me keep going.

Then one day I was completely blindsided by generosity. I walked to my mailbox as usual and grabbed a stack of mail from inside. Slowly sauntering back to the door, I flipped through the junk and bills, only to find one plain white envelope with no return address. I opened it and inside found a check with my name on it!

Standing there on my front porch, I was dumbfounded! Who was this anonymous stranger? Where did this gift come from?

Tears ran down my cheeks, and I felt deeply grateful.

And at that moment I knew what I needed to do. You see, money is like a river. It's meant to keep on moving.

I remember slipping a twenty-dollar bill in the office mailbox of a woman who volunteered at our church. It wasn't much, but I knew it could help. Her husband had left her, and she was struggling to find a job and to care for her children.

It felt so good to be able to do a little something for someone else out of the generosity that had been shown to me.

And the checks continued to arrive. Month after month for six years, I'd find that unmarked envelope in my mailbox—enough to help me, enough to help someone else.

When I told Carol about my anonymous donor and what I'd been doing with the money, she laughed. As it turned out, one of her other clients was my benefactor, and Carol was the sly sleuth who had provided my address. Knowing how he and his family supported me, she'd been offering him free haircuts for the last six years.

One day I finally met the man who had been writing

those checks. I couldn't believe it! I'm so grateful for him and his family. And I'm thankful not only for those envelopes. I'm also thankful that, because of their generosity, I can participate in generosity.

Because they give, I can give.

I LIKE FIRST CLASS: MATT

One of the perks of flying as much as I do is that occasionally I get a free upgrade to first class. The priority boarding and extra legroom are definitely a plus, but my favorite part of sitting up front is getting a complimentary beverage as soon as I sit down. I like to stay hydrated when I fly, so any opportunity to avoid airport prices for a bottle of water is definitely a bonus.

On this particular morning I was flying out of a smaller airport and had been awarded a free upgrade. It was business as usual as I sat writing e-mails in the boarding area until I noticed a man nearby who was blind. I watched as the gate agent explained the boarding process to him, and I felt a desire to give my first-class seat to him.

The thought wouldn't leave me alone. I sat there for a few minutes just thinking it through. I deserved this first-class seat, didn't I? I fly a lot, so the occasional upgrade is the least they can do for me, right? It would be too awkward to approach a stranger and offer him my seat, wouldn't it? And let's not forget that free bottle of water I was looking forward to once aboard.

Despite the scores of hesitations crowding into my head, I wanted to do it. Deciding to be discreet, I approached the gate agent and explained what I had in mind. He was surprised and thanked me several times while he made the switch, giving me an exit-row window seat—one of the best seats in coach.

I was allowed to board early, so I got to walk through first class and see the recipient of my gift sitting happily in his seat. Being the first person on board in the economy cabin, I had a few minutes to sit and think before the rest of the plane boarded.

It was then that a sense of gratitude really sank in.

Yes, gratitude. It was as if the act of giving had opened me up to realize all the ways I am blessed.

I typically give away at least 50 percent of what I earn, but in that moment I realized I could never give away even close to 50 percent of all the blessings I've received in my life. The upgrade had been given to me for free, after all, and while many people go their entire lives without flying, I get to travel to many amazing places and meet many great people.

I felt profoundly aware of all the good things in my life, and any sense of entitlement melted away. I sat in silence, realizing that giving away my first-class seat had been much more rewarding than sitting in it myself.

To top it off, the flight attendant gave me a free bottle of water when I sat down after all!

●●●

Matt gave away his comfortable seat, but he received more than he gave.

Two of the big barriers to living generously are the beliefs that we are owed something by the world and that, compared to others, we don't have anything to give. If you think that way, let me ask you a question: Are you breathing? You would not be able to read this if someone had not nurtured you when you were a baby, if someone had not taught you to read when you were young. Take a minute to think of a few of the many things you have been given in your life. Chances are we have all been loved by someone and have all been shown generosity. If we hadn't, we likely wouldn't be alive today.

I realize that some people's lives are harder than others. If you've been dealt a bad hand, I understand. Even in the United States where equality is one of our chief values, inequality is still rampant.

But focusing on what you don't have or the bad hand you were dealt can actually make your life worse. What you think about affects who you become. It affects your relationships and the people you attract into your life. Keeping your focus on what you do have, what you have been given, and the good things in your life will make you happier and more grateful and will empower you to become a generous person yourself.

Trust me, I've had bad things come my way. Who hasn't?

I've been through some incredibly hard times, financially and relationally. What I've found is that taking my eyes off my problems and giving to others has helped me recover and heal. I believe it will do the same for you.

Some people hear the I Like Giving stories and say, "Well, that could never be me. I'm in debt, my bills are too high, and I don't earn enough money." I don't know all the details of your situation, but I can tell you this: giving to others will help you no matter where you are in life. Give and it will be given to you. Sow and you will reap. If you give to others, it will come back to you in unexpected ways.

Remember, giving is for you—it gives you life.

I'm not suggesting you neglect yourself for the sake of helping other people. What I am saying is that I believe we are made in the image of a God whose very nature is to give. If you focus on what you lack, you might find yourself lonely and miserable. If you focus instead on what you have been given and how you can give to others, you might start becoming the type of person that people gather around and take notice of when you are in a hard time. We don't give to get, but giving fosters healthy relationships, and we all need those whether we are in a hard time or not.

Elizabeth Dunn and Michael Norton, two of the researchers we mentioned earlier, note that giving both time and money can make us feel like we have more. Not only does donating time make you feel as if you have more time, but giving away as little as one dollar can make you feel wealthier.

A while back I was going through a hard time financially. I had very little to cover my expenses; I was under a lot of stress. Still, I wanted to keep giving. When you purpose in your heart to give to others, you sometimes discover resources you didn't even know you had.

During that time, for me, giving took the form of an alligator riding a unicycle.

Yes, you read that right. I have an eccentric uncle who gave me the idea to buy an unusual piece of art—a sculpture of an alligator riding a unicycle. It sat in my office and was a great conversation piece. But when I was in a pinch financially, wondering how to keep giving, I realized that I really didn't need it anymore. I sold it and gave all the money away.

How many times have you needed money for something and found a way to make it work? When there is no other option, solutions have a way of showing up.

What if giving wasn't optional for you? Perhaps you would realize you have a few things in your life that you could sell or give away. If you're absolutely broke, maybe you can lend someone a hand. Maybe you can give the gift of time, a smile, or a listening ear. If there is life and breath in you and you want to give, you can find a way. The possibilities are endless.

At this point you might be wondering, *Isn't this chapter about receiving?*

Well, yes, it is, but one of the beautiful things you'll see on your journey is that the lines between giving and receiving disappear. You might see yourself as a giver in one situation but realize that the blessing you receive from giving is so great that you are really the receiver.

Giving and receiving are two sides of the same coin.

Receiving can be scary because we have less control. When we are in the position to give to someone else, we can decide when and how to do it. We can even change our minds if we want to. When we are in the position of receiving, we control none of those things.

A few years ago a friend who served as a youth pastor at a church in our city died in a fire along with his infant son. His wife and their two little girls were away visiting her parents and heard the news from afar. I can't imagine anything more difficult than losing your mate and your child unexpectedly. Words fall short of doing any justice to that level of tragedy, and yet, Charity shares the experience with great courage.

I LIKE PEOPLE: CHARITY

"Your house is on fire."

These were the words that woke me just after midnight. I was not home. I was far from it and safe, nestled snugly in the sheets in my parent's guest bedroom, my two young girls beside me, breathing deeply. But my house, the one where my husband and five-month-old son slept that night, had been spewing smoke for hours before my neighbor realized it and contacted me.

How I wished to know everything! How I wanted to

stop this story that was unfolding before me. But I was more than a thousand miles away, with plans to take my girls to Disney World to spin wild in the teacups.

My mind was racing as I frantically called everyone I knew in an effort to find out what was happening and whether my husband and my baby had survived. Since it was the middle of the night, no one answered. I went on Google and typed in my address. Live news articles flashed across my screen, confirming this existential horror.

"House on fire."

"Infant rushed to ER."

"Man in cardiac arrest."

I finally got hold of someone who worked in the hospital's ER. The horrifying words echoed through the phone: "I'm really sorry, but your baby passed."

I hung up in disbelief.

My phone rang. My father-in-law. His voice broke as he told me that his son, my husband, the one who was washing dishes in the sink just hours ago, had not survived.

I wasn't sure how I would either.

I quickly bundled up my girls, grabbed my luggage, and caught a flight home. But I had no home. It was a charred mess. And I had no husband to hold me tight. I felt a galaxy away from normal.

Later, when I stood facing the caskets, I remembered a time years earlier, though it felt like yesterday, when my brother was buried after the car accident that took his life. I was already in town that day because I was visiting my dad in the hospital. He had also been in a major car accident. My dad, who had made it to the funeral on a gurney, took the mike and said, "This is the day the LORD has made. We will rejoice and be glad in it." The audience sat like statues. I wondered if these words were possible. I gripped the tissue tight.

When my husband, Derek, and I met, we spent a lot of time talking about who we wanted to be. We knew, even after my brother's funeral, that we wanted our lives to be about joy, come what may. We wanted to experience joy in the good and choose joy in the bad. I knew I needed to find my way back to this joy, and I was going to need a lot of help.

Fortunately, my whole life I have been a "collector of people." Circling around me were friends old and young, near and far. There were childhood friends, the ones who ran barefoot with me through the meadow on our 160-acre farm. There were church friends, the ones we shared our hearts with when we built a new church from the ground up. There were family members and neighbors and coworkers and college buddies—many of whom had shared meals around our table before it burned.

When I was completely overtaken by grief, these people stepped in to make a way for me to move forward. People brought meals, mailed cards, donated vacation time, cared for my girls, and made space so I could care for myself. Then they dug deeper and said, "We're gonna build you a house."

Fund-raisers began, fliers were posted, charity golf outings were held, and marathons were run. People said things like, "I'm going to buy your floors," "I'm going to buy your cabinets." When the frames went up, people came over to write words of hope on the two-by-fours.

I was drenched in love.

Not once did I need to ask for anything.

When Derek and I were in school studying business, we always said the best return on investment comes from investing in people. The return is immeasurable. We usually think about giving in financial terms, and in my case that certainly happened, but it was people's time and emotions that meant the most. Generosity reaches far beyond a wallet. My gratitude for this generosity rescued me from my despair.

When I sit at my table and break bread, I wish those two empty chairs were filled. I miss my husband and my son and the way things were. But I look around my house and remember that I am not alone. I don't see bricks and curtains; I see people.

I see beauty from ashes.

●●●

The truth is we are not in control of much of anything in life. Charity's story is hard to read because it was an unimaginably difficult experience for her and her family.

But for all the tragedy, her story is also a poignant example of what generosity, community, and receiving can do in the midst of some of life's hardest moments. Charity and her husband, Derek, had surrounded themselves with a community that they invested their lives in. Because they did, Charity was not alone when disaster struck. Her community came around her without anyone asking and poured their lives out for her.

Often when we see someone in a bad situation, our natural response is to say, "Hey, if you need anything, let me know." Please don't say that. Unknowingly you have put an added burden on the person. For some people the pressure is just too great, so they freeze and never respond.

It's a dangerous comment that produces a false sense of doing good. I encourage you to assess the situation and make something happen.

Charity's story reminds us how precious life is and how hard life can be. If you get stuck in the head space of thinking that you have nothing to give or that you've been dealt a bad hand, remember there are almost certainly other people who are worse off than you. If you've lost everything and have nothing but the shirt on your back, you still have a lot to give. In fact, you can choose to live your entire life as a gift, whether you feel as if you have a lot to offer or not. Live to give, and you will be surprised at the resources you have. Let those resources flow through your life like a river, and watch as the water level rises. Life is meant to be given away, and as you give, more will be given to you.

I LIKE
BEING ROBBED.

Submitted by: Steve

It was my morning to open. On the short drive to the shop, I was asking God for a strong day in sales. Like many new business owners, we were struggling to pay bills. This week was especially tight.

I arrived at the coffee shop at 5:30 a.m., unlocked the door, and proceeded to walk behind the counter. Noticing the open cash drawer, my first thought was, *Why did Chris leave it open?*

In the next instant I saw why. The floor under the drawer was strewn with miscellaneous items from the shop—a knife with its blade broken off, an airpot with the bottom dented in, change from the drawer (mostly pennies), and the twisted remains of our iPad counter stand.

Apparently after failed attempts with a knife and an airpot, someone had used the iPad stand to pry open the cash drawer. The reality sank in.

I'd been robbed. There was $200 cash missing, along with the rolled-coin change bag with another $100. So minutes after my prayer for a strong day, we were $300 in the hole to start the morning.

A call to 911 brought instructions not to touch anything.

I got coffee going while waiting for the sheriff's department to show up. I had to open to avoid losing sales. My sons and nephew, our barista team, showed up to help.

The police came and investigated while the boys and I waited on customers. My heart was heavy with the loss of the cash, but I continued to greet customers with a half smile.

At 9:15 one of our regular customers, who had been in earlier, walked back into the shop and ordered a coffee. I prepared it and rang him up. Just before he left, he pushed an envelope across the counter.

I asked, "What's this?"

He replied, "It's for you." Then he walked out the door.

I opened the envelope, and there in ten-, five-, and one-dollar bills and rolls of coins was $300. I learned later that he knew we had been robbed.

Yet he had no idea how much had been taken.

Tears filled my eyes as I recognized this as a gift from God, who knows our needs and heard my prayer and spoke to the heart of our customer.

The next day the gift giver came back in, and I shared with him how timely his gift was and how it was an answer to a prayer I'd prayed on my way to work.

His response: "I just did what God prompted me to do."

God didn't have to answer this way, but on that morning he chose to encourage our hearts and remind us that he knows our needs—right down to the exact penny.

11

BECOMING
A GIFT

Do you wake up every morning excited about a new day? Do you live each day with anticipation, expectation, and energy? Do you go to bed at night feeling satisfied, happy, and glad to be alive? Do you have a sense that you make the world a better place and that you are the only person in the world who could be you and do what you do? If so, you've probably discovered the transforming power of a generous life. If not, your life is about to change.

We're not made to serve ourselves. Have you noticed that if you have only enough time and energy to focus on yourself, life just isn't that great? Have you experienced that amazing feeling of realizing that someone just did something for you without even being asked? Have you tasted the joy that comes from doing the same thing for others?

When generosity becomes your lifestyle, your life will

take on a new glow. You will feel appreciated. You will feel worthy. You will feel celebrated, and you will get that deep sense of satisfaction that comes from knowing you enrich other people's lives. When giving moves from being an occasional activity to the very essence of your life, you start experiencing the fullness of life at a whole different level.

When your goal is to live your life as a gift, you move from asking how you can get ahead to how you can serve others to the best of your ability. The question is not "What am I good at?" but "How can I best give my life away to others?" The University of Rochester professors found that people with life goals that focused on giving to others became happier as they met those goals, while people with self-focused goals got, if anything, less happy even if they were very successful.

What would becoming a gift in every area of your life look like? If you ask yourself that question and begin living your life as a gift, you will discover satisfaction beyond anything you have known before.

My friend Mark Batterson moved from Chicago to Washington DC to serve with a small church. Since then the church has grown exponentially, and he has started a coffeehouse on Capitol Hill, which continues to bring people together in that community.

I LIKE TRUCKS: MARK

I was looking at the checkbook balance. It wasn't zero, but I could sure see it from where I stood.

We were trying to launch a new ministry. It was a major stretch of faith, especially financially. Money was tight, and it wasn't pouring in.

Establishing a new ministry in Washington DC was slow going at first. We had a number of financial challenges. However, even in our tight circumstances, my wife and I shared the real sense that we needed to donate to a group that was starting up about the same time we were. It was focusing on the significant needs that exist within the blocks and miles around the US Capitol.

Believe it or not, there are nearly seven thousand homeless people and fifty-seven thousand people in extreme poverty in the Washington DC area. With stats like that, we felt we needed to do something.

That's why we wrote the check. It wasn't much by many standards—$350—but it was a lot for us then, a real stretch of faith. I think we often look at the great needs in the world and see all the things we can't do, which keeps us from doing the things we can do.

I went to the post office and dropped the envelope in the mailbox outside, then went inside to check our post office box. Imagine how shocked I was when I opened an envelope that contained a $10,000 check to support our ministry! We don't believe in giving to get, but it was an amazing surprise.

The money we gave back then was used to buy a truck to help the homeless and hungry, and what's cool is that I still see it around DC all the time. I love it. It's like, "Hey, there goes our investment!" and it gives us a great deal of joy to know our giving has played a role over the years in helping so many people in our city.

Being generous is an attitude. We have opportunities around us all the time. As for me and my family—well, we've gone from loving to give to living to give.

● ● ●

Mark is one of those friends who inspire me by their servant attitude and their boldness in living lives of service to others. He is also one of the most energetic and alive people I have ever met. I honestly believe he gets out of bed every morning feeling energized by the awareness that his life makes a difference to others. I think that's a feeling we can all have.

You don't have to make massive life changes, move to another city, or start your own nonprofit to become a gift to other people. You can start with who you are, right where you are, right now. In fact, you probably are already a gift to many people in many ways, but you might not always be aware of it.

Mark says, "We need to change our routine, take some risks, and try new things. And if we do, we will find ourselves coming alive again."[9] Perhaps a few small changes in your routine are enough to revolutionize your life.

Take a minute to think about it. How do you view your job? Do you see it as a way to earn a paycheck, or do you take pride in knowing that your company serves its customers well and that you, in turn, serve your company well? Do you ask yourself how your unique gifts and abilities could serve others better? Do you find yourself getting happier as you reach your goals, or do you live with a sense of dissatisfaction?

What about your personal life? Do you see yourself as a gift to your family, your friends, your community? Do you feel frustrated that life isn't what you want it to be, or do you take joy in finding new ways to contribute and give?

What about your leisure time? How could you make that more generous? Would teaching your kids to fish be more satisfying than going fishing by yourself? Could volunteering at a local charity be more life giving than sitting on your couch watching television?

Remember—there is no obligation here. These questions should not make you feel bad about how you currently live. See them as presenting opportunities to live an even better life than you already do while improving the lives of those around you. Refocusing any aspect of your life through the lens of generosity can be an exceptionally powerful way to do both.

Once you start asking the right questions, those questions can lead to the right answers. Perhaps you are not well suited for your job; maybe moving to a different career would free you up to become a better gift to others. If that is the case, moving will benefit everyone. Finding your place in the world and becoming the gift that only you can become is a good thing to want to do—it's best for everyone.

So take a moment, wherever you are, whatever your life circumstances are, and ask yourself, "How can my life become a gift?"

Think it through. Ask your friends. Make a list of the ways you give and how you can grow in generosity. Add to your list little by little. You don't have to be a millionaire to give, and you don't have to have a lot of money to be rich.

All you have to do is start living to give.

I LIKE
PEACE.

Submitted by: Mike

The court had spoken, and it was settled as far as I was concerned. No point in revisiting past battles.

The divorce had been contentious and a strain on everyone, especially my kids, who were teenagers at the time. My ex-wife had received a handsome settlement but had squandered it through the years. That was close to thirty years ago. It wasn't my issue that she was struggling.

Or so I thought.

The fact that the courts had settled it decades ago didn't matter to my second wife, Ann, to whom I've now been married twenty-six years.

"We need to do something for her," she said to me. "I can't keep telling your children I love them and yet not take care of their mother."

The statement shocked me. My initial reply was, "It's not my problem," but the reality of Ann's statement and the compassion behind it planted a seed in my soul I couldn't shake. The more it germinated, the more God broke down my resistance. I had a real sense that he was saying to me, "You may have settled this in a human court, but you never settled it in my court."

It took a couple of years, but as my heart and mind transitioned from an earthly court's ruling to a spiritual realm where God's grace is abundant, I knew Ann was right.

We needed to do something.

But what? Control issues were a significant problem

in my previous marriage and part of what had driven us to divorce court. If Ann and I didn't approach the offer to help in the right way, it could make things worse. We talked to my kids—all adults now—and together we decided they would approach her with the offer to help as a gift from all of us, which it was. We wanted to buy her a house.

God is good! He prepared her heart to receive the offer. She was grateful. She confessed her concerns about the future. Even though we told her she was open to use whichever Realtor she wanted and to live wherever she wanted, she agreed to use the one we'd been using to research costs and locations.

Ann and I wrote the check on closing day, and as the attorney was handing us the keys, I said, "No, those belong to her. It is her house."

The people working on the closing couldn't understand why we would do such a thing, but I can honestly say we have never experienced more joy than in providing her a place to live. I'm convinced the joy comes from being obedient to what God wants.

We've learned through the years that generosity has intangible and tangible benefits. I sold my business fifteen years ago, and I tell people that Ann and I are not retired— we're available.

That idea really hit us when Ann asked a young Russian student if she was concerned about returning to Russia. Ann had been helping the student while she was in the United States. Since it was the early 1990s and financially very difficult in Russia, Ann wondered if the student might not want to go home. The student's candid response shook our world: "No, I would never want to be like you Americans. You spend all your time taking care of your things."

Wow! That statement changed our lifestyle. We started downsizing everything. We began to truly believe that God owns it all anyway. It is his. That comment opened a whole new world to us—a lifestyle of generosity.

Even though Ann's statement about helping my ex-wife initially shocked me, I'm not surprised that she was sensitive to this opportunity. The process has again proved that most often generosity benefits the giver as much or more than the receiver. The process of buying the house brought a significant amount of healing between my former spouse and me and between us and our children. They used to be very protective of their mother—and rightfully so—but they are much more relaxed now because they know their mother is being taken care of.

It's been nearly eight years since she received the house, and the relationships among all of us have been open and friendly.

Here's a better way to say it: now there is true peace in our family.

12

A GENEROUS WORLD

By now you have seen the power of a simple act of generosity.

Every time we give, a story begins, and the rippling effects of one simple act are immeasurable.

Giving has been an incredibly transformative experience for me. As I have practiced this more and more, I have found myself more connected and sympathetic to the people around me. I wake up every morning wondering if the day will give me a chance to participate in another person's life in some way. When the opportunity comes my way, I feel sincerely grateful that it did. I give not only because giving brings me joy but also because there is deep satisfaction in knowing I have helped another person. Few things in the world feel as good and as right as giving.

Generosity has made me more aware of the needs of

others and given me the freedom to ask myself, "Could I help them with that?" I don't ask from the standpoint of obligation—"*Should* I do something about that?"—but as an opportunity—"Do I *get* to do something about this?" I can't give what I don't have. I can give only what I do have, and I get excited about that.

There are a lot of problems in the world. Sitting around talking about them or waiting for a large organization to do something about them doesn't work. Finding opportunities to help others and change the world around us does work. We just have to take that scary step of actually doing something. We don't need to overthink what we do. Sometimes we just know this is our opportunity to help. When we recognize an opportunity and dive in, amazing things happen!

What if the more than 315 million Americans alive today would do something generous for someone else daily, weekly, or even monthly. How powerful could that be? What type of impact would that have on our country and the world? What if everyone in the world started living more generously? How much healthier, happier, and more connected would we all be?

Could small acts of generosity have a massive impact on the world? I believe they could. I believe they do.

So the question then becomes, are we willing? Will we decide to live generously and then be open to the opportunities that come our way? Being willing is where it starts. Once you decide you are willing, you will become aware of the opportunities around you, and then all you have to do is act. One person at a time, one opportunity at a time, is all it takes. And no matter who you are or where you live, you can give.

This book is just the start. Once you put it down, the adventure really begins. Giving stories are like us—all unique. I predict that as you give, your life will become so filled with adventure and stories that you won't be able to remember them all!

At I Like Giving we want to journey with you as you embrace the generous life. We've created resources at ILikeGiving.com and www.facebook.com/ilikegiving so we can encourage you often and always. I invite you to join our growing community by signing up for I Like Giving updates at ILikeGiving.com/join-us. You'll find fresh stories to read and inspiring videos. We'd also love to hear your stories, so we have created a way for you to submit them to us online. We think this book is just the first of many, so when we write our next book, we hope your story will be in it too!

A while back a story came to us that astounded me. Tim, a businessman in Oklahoma City, woke up one morning and told himself that he would look for an opportunity to help someone that day. Later as he was on his way home from the store, he noticed a man on the side of the road with a flat tire. Realizing this was his chance, he pulled over. The man with the flat tire, Jerry, had loaned his spare tire to a friend that same morning and was stuck. Tim offered to take him to a store to get a new tire. On the way his story started to unfold.

Jerry had moved to Oklahoma City looking for a new life. He'd lived out of his van for two months and had taken jobs making balloon animals for kids and washing dishes at four different restaurants. He was barely getting by.

Tim ended up taking Jerry back to his apartment so he could change and get to one of his jobs on time. When Tim asked Jerry what his dream job would look like, he quickly responded, "I love the idea of selling something!"

Tim then took Jerry to work and called a tow truck to pick up his car. When the guys at the tire store heard Jerry's story, they all chipped in to give him a discount.

He was back on the road the next morning.

The next day Tim was fishing with his friend Bill and mentioned his encounter with Jerry. Bill, who owns a Chevrolet dealership, asked Tim if he thought Jerry could be good at sales.

He smiled as he recalled Jerry's response the day before. "Yes, I believe he has what it takes to be great at sales," he replied.

Jerry got an interview at the dealership a few days later and was hired on the spot.

Today he is the number-two salesman in the whole dealership. He's driving a much more reliable car and doesn't have to stretch himself between multiple jobs just to scrape by. If Jerry hadn't shown kindness to his friend that one morning by lending him his spare tire, if Tim hadn't decided to pull over and help, and if he had not been willing to inconvenience himself to help Jerry out of a hard situation, Jerry might still be where he was before. Because they each chose to give, a remarkable chain of events came together that has changed both of their lives.

That is the power of choosing to give.

So as you read these final paragraphs and put down this book, you will be left with two choices. One is to continue living your life just as you have been. Perhaps you can't imagine your life getting any better. Perhaps you are already doing everything you possibly can to make the world a better place.

But if you have any sense that your life might not be everything you'd like it to be, if you know that you could live more generously and embrace the adventure of giving to others, then I challenge you to go out and do something about it.

If you embrace generosity as a way of life, I predict that years from now you'll look back and be amazed at how your life has changed. You'll know then that this one decision—the decision to give—has profoundly altered your own story. And you will feel a real connection between your story and the stories of the people around you. Choosing to live your life as a gift offers you not only the best life possible but also the possibility of being part of creating a generous world—the best world for all of us.

So why not put this book down, take a look at the world around you, and make the choice to give? Give often, give in a thousand different ways, and enjoy living your life as a gift. It's the best choice for you, and it's the best choice for all of us.

WAYS TO SPREAD THE JOY

Here are a few ways you can use this book to share these inspiring stories and keep the generosity ripple going!

- Host a community group with the new I Like Giving Small Group Experience, available for purchase at shopilikegiving.com.

    Past small group participants are saying, "Discussing stories of generosity is something I've never done before. It's so life giving!"

- Give the book to your employer, employees, pastor, and favorite charities.

- Give the book to board members of organizations you're connected with.

- Give the book as a gift to donors of your organization, church, or nonprofit.

- Invite the author to speak at your church, business or event by emailing brad1@ilikegiving.com.

ACKNOWLEDGMENTS

I give thanks to the Lord, who gave me the gift of all gifts in Jesus.

Also, thanks to my wife, Laura, and our three children—Danny, Drew, and Gracie. I will never forget our family prayer as we agreed to write this book and your willingness to give up time playing catch, going to the lake, and hearing some bedtime stories to make it happen.

I am grateful for Iain Cook, who returned from Hawaii on a wild-goose chase to help take words from my mouth and land them on these pages. And for the team at Baas Creative, whose creative process is perfection. The cover and premier stories are genius.

My thanks to everyone who submitted stories for this book. Your generosity continues to live!

To Ken Petersen for the brilliance of creating a solid foundation for the work before one word was written. To Claire Gibson, Blair Moore, Chris Turner, and Carolyn Baas for assembling works of art called giving stories. And to the one and only Esther Fedorkevich. Your heart and stick-to-it-iveness through the entire project make me want to write another one!

To Stanley Tam, for your challenge to journal stories seven years ago so that one day I would write a book.

ACKNOWLEDGMENTS

To Carol Bartley for showing up at the perfect time in the editing process. And many thanks to the team at WaterBrook Multnomah, who all had a hand in bringing this book to life.

NOTES

1. Kent M. Keith, "The Paradoxical Commandments." Used by permission.
2. Elizabeth Dunn and Michael Norton, *Happy Money: The Science of Smarter Spending* (New York: Simon & Schuster, 2013).
3. Daniel H. Pink, *Drive: The Surprising Truth About What Motivates Us* (New York: Riverhead, 2011).
4. Stephen Post and Jill Neimark, *Why Good Things Happen to Good People: How to Live a Longer, Healthier, Happier Life by the Simple Act of Giving* (New York: Broadway, 2008), 1.
5. Post and Neimark, *Why Good Things Happen*, 2.
6. Post and Neimark, *Why Good Things Happen*, 7.
7. Henri Nouwen, *The Return of the Prodigal Son: A Story of Homecoming* (New York: Doubleday, 1992), 131.
8. Leigh Anne Tuohy and Sean Tuohy with Sally Jenkins, *In a Heartbeat: Sharing the Power of Cheerful Giving* (New York: Henry Holt, 2010), 22.
9. Mark Batterson, *Wild Goose Chase: Reclaim the Adventure of Pursuing God* (Colorado Springs, CO: Multnomah, 2008), 44.

I LIKE _____

_____

_____

_____

_____

_____

_____

_____

_____

_____

_____

_____

_____

_____

_____

_____

_____

I LIKE _____

_____

_____

_____

_____

_____

_____

_____

_____

_____

_____

_____

_____

_____

_____

_____

_____

_____

_____

I LIKE _____

_____

_____

_____

_____

_____

_____

_____

_____

_____

_____

_____

_____

_____

_____

_____

1. Did you feel free from any sense of duty or obligation when you gave? If so, how did that affect how you felt about the experience?

_____

_____

_____

_____

_____

_____

_____

_____

_____

_____

_____

_____

_____

_____

2. Were you surprised by how many people or opportunities came your way? Do you think the world changed, or do you think your perspective did?

_____

_____

_____

_____

_____

_____

_____

_____

_____

_____

_____

_____

_____

_____

3. Now that you've discovered the joy of giving (or re-discovered it), how does that affect how you think about your life? Are there opportunities for you to give that you hadn't noticed before? How can you grow in giving to others?

_____

_____

_____

_____

_____

_____

_____

_____

_____

_____

_____

_____

_____

ABOUT THE AUTHOR

Brad Formsma is the founder and president of ILikeGiving.com, a movement that has inspired more than 100 million people worldwide to live generously. In addition to the online movement, I Like Giving works with churches and businesses to create healthy cultures through generosity. Brad has been featured on *Today*, *Fox News*, *National Geographic*, and *Forbes*. He speaks  on leadership and organizational health for sales teams and businesses, including Trek Bicycle, Southeastern Freight Lines, Merrill Lynch, and Johns Hopkins. He also guides families through custom gatherings to help them discuss generosity together with every generation, so that their values and stories live on. Brad lives in Southern California with his wife, Laura, and their three children.

For speaking requests,
please visit
bradformsma.com.

Check out Brad's newest book
Everyday Generosity: Becoming a Generous Family in a Selfie World

Co-authored with his son Drew, together they will encourage you to become a generous family at every age and stage.

To learn more and order your copy visit www.everydaygenerosity.com

I Like Giving resources for your church and business

Business

Better teamwork, better employees, better business.

Research shows that generosity makes business better.

- Refreshed™: A series of stories emailed to your team at
the pace that works best for you

- Inspirational speaking for keynote, staff, and board events

- I Like Giving books for your business

Church

Infuse a lifestyle of generosity into your congregation with
I Like Giving:

- 3-week "I Like Giving" sermon series

- Refreshed™: A series of giving stories sent to your church
to inspire generous living

- "I Like Giving: The Small Group Experience"

- Discounted I Like Giving books for your church

Bring I Like Giving to your church and business.
Learn more at Illkegiving.com